THEMES, SCHEMES AND DREAMS

BY

PATTY SACHS

Your Special Event, Inc.

Weddings, Parties and Celebrations
by Patty Sachs

Copyright © 1990 Your Special Event, Inc.
35 Nathan Lane, #309
Plymouth, MN 55405

Printed in The United States of America

ISBN 0-9616680-2-4

Credits:

Author and Publisher: Patty Sachs
Associate Publisher: Scott Bachman
Chief Editor: Kelly Ryan
Project Director: Roni Brunner
Cover Design: Don Stewart
Book Design and Typesetting: Bob Gordon
Printer: Printing Solutions
Graphics: Sheri Bethke
Proofreading: Corky Adams, Dan Desmond, Cathy
Sachs, Janet Steinberg

Dedication

I dedicate this book to a great lady, Elsie Iverson, who is my mom and my friend. Her spirit, spunk, sense of humor and loyal support of all my endeavors. I celebrate her every day. She has backed me up all my life.

I also dedicate this book to my darling grand-daughter, Jasmine Jenee (Ta Ta W.) who has been my social life, my love life, my security and sanity for the past eight months. I celebrate her every day. She has kept me up all of her life.

Acknowledgements

My love and thanks to the following:

Kelly Ryan and Gil Quesada (The Administrator) for being good and loving friends. For thinking that I am the best thing since helium and constantly telling me so.

My children, Frank, Cathy (Foosie) and Deena for thinking that I am the best thing since The Bank of America, even though I am not like other moms. I love them for caring enough to say "I told you so" and yet, caring enough to cheer me on.

Roni Brunner for ending all of my sentences for me, being the tough guy now and then and cheerfully being my co-queen of "Ca Ca". This book could not have been written with out her commitment.

Bob Gordon for supporting me in my endeavor, going above and beyond even though I am way behind.

Jan F., Stelle F., Kathy L., Susan T., Jackie C., Karen R., Ron G., Dee S., Lynda O., Steve C., Shirlee C., Barbara E.for still being there for me, though I have been unavailable for almost one year.

My sister, Laurie, my brothers and sisters-in law, Art & Carol, Terry and Binky, Bill and Scott for giving me the opportunity to try out all of my party skills on them for hundreds of special occasions.

The clients who have allowed me to be as good for them as I wanted to be That is how I learned most of what I know.

Patty Sachs

Mother: Frank, Cathy and Deena

Grandmother: Jasmine Jenee

Entertainer: Twin Cities Nightclubs

Inventor: Coupons Ala Cart, coupon file box that attaches to shopping cart

Innovator: Weight Loss Closet, consignment shop for dieting women

Columnist: Balloons and Parties Today, Great Events, Global Meetings, Apartment Directory

Writer/Director: Variety Shows,The Law Revue

Songwriter: Custom songs for own company, Song Sendsations, Inc.

Special Event Planner: For own company, Your Special Event, Inc.

Trade Show Producer: Your Special Event Trade Show, 1987, Event Expo '90, 1990

Author: Twin Cities Party Guide and Directory, 1986

Your Special Event Planning Guide, 1988

Weddings, Parties and Celebrations, 1990

Shower Singer: Third Place, Coast to Coast Shower Singing Contest

Introduction

Much to my mother's discomfort, I was born wearing a teeny, sparkly, pointed party hat, fake nose and glasses. Some babies cry at birth, I tossed confetti around the delivery room. It seemed appropriate, since I was born on my mom's birthday. Sharing our birthdays has its advantages. I never forget Mom on her special day. I have forgotten other important details, though

Those of us who are blessed with party fever begin competing at an early age for the title of "hostess with the mostest". My official debut came in first grade when I invited some of my classmates to a small get-together. It was just kicking off when one of the guests suggested, "After the party, let's go to the park." My mom said, "Oh, are you girls going to a party?" Seems I'd overlooked one pesky detail--informing Mom that I was having a party. Enter the original Perle "Mestup."

An inauspicious beginning perhaps, but it grew into a long and active career of party planning, as a hostess and as a helpful guest. Hundreds of cakes in all shapes and colors, most of them ordered from the local bakery at the last minute. My favorite party cake was also a personal best in bargain hunting (one of my other favorite pastimes.) For my parents 25th anniversary I grabbed up a "goof" sheet cake for next to nothing. It said, "Happy Bar Mitzvah, Melvin!" I had the baker cross out Mel's greeting and write "Happy Anniversary Mom and Dad, You know I could never resist a bargain."

As the oldest of six children, with both parents working, I was the official Easter Bunny, Santa Claus, Pumpkin carver, Tree trimmer, Valentine Cutter, gift wrapper, crepe paper twister, balloon blower-upper, Forth of July firecracker monitor, surrogate Birthday party Mom, costume maker, cake baker and offical family representative to weddings and showers.

I've instigated and pulled off over a hundred surprise parties and amazingly enough, I've been surprised three time, myself. My real passion is a costume party.

In 1982 I began to plan parties for money. Never knowing that someday I would have accumulated enough knowledge and expertise to be able to write three books. It is lucky that I accumulated the know-how, it made up for the high prices I paid to people for letting me work for them. (Once a volunteer, the mind-set dies hard.)

My first two books were written for the folks in the Twin Cities area, and there was some serious partying here. This book will be sold all over the country. There are only two kinds of people that should read this book, though. Those that plan and give weddings, parties and celebrations and those that go to weddings, parties and celebrations.

As I sit here, about to become a nationally recognized party girl, I am wearing my sparkly, pointed party hat, my fake nose and glasses. I'm ready for a celebration. I have made some great progress though, since, this time I told Mom.

TABLE OF CONTENTS

Preface: The Cake Concept

1. The Event: What Makes It Special?   1

2. Special People: Make Events Special   5

3. The Plan: Creating the Cake   9
    Notes & Numbers   14

4. The Theme: The Common Bond   15

5. Theme Ideas:
    (A)rabian Nights to (Z)orba's Dance   22

6. The Schedule:
    The Minute by Minute Waltz   30

7. The Space: Let's Not Build A Barn   36
    Notes & Numbers   43

8. Unique Sites: (A)trium to (Z)oo   44
    Notes & Numbers   52

9. The Budget: Expert Rationalization   53
    Notes & Numbers   59

10. Invitations: Offers They Can't Refuse   60
    Notes & Numbers   82

11. Entertainment: The Life of the Party   84
    Notes & Numbers   92

12. Guest Comfort: Are We Having Fun Yet?   94
    Notes & Numbers   106

13. Celebration Clothes:
    All Dressed Up with Someplace to Go   107
    Notes & Numbers   115

14. Name tags/Place cards: Anxiety Busters   116
　　　　Notes & Numbers   121

15. Decorations: Balloons, Bouquets, Banners 122
　　　　Notes & Numbers   131

16. Photo/Video: Lights, Camera, Interaction 133

17. Sentimentality:
　　Memories, Wishes, Blessings   134

18. Holiday Stress: Don't Worry..be Happier   140

19. Party Pooling:
　　Punch Bowls to Piano Players   146
　　　　Notes & Numbers   152

20. Economy Events: Penny Wise Parties   153
　　　　Notes & Numbers   160

21. Fund Raisers: Benefits, Balls, Ball Games 161

22. Buffets/Bars:
　　Here's Where We Draw the Line   166

23. 90's Trends: Fun in our Future   179

24. Gifts:
　　For People Who Deserve Everything   185
　　　　Notes & Numbers   191

25. The Planner: Hassle-Free Hosting   193
　　　　Notes & Numbers   199

26. Kids Parties: They're Party People, Too   200
　　　　Notes & Numbers   206

27. The Experts:
　　Rentals,Caterers,Transportation   207

28. Shower Ideas: Bridal and Baby Bashes   219
      Notes & Numbers   226

29. Planning Resources: Read 'em and Reap   227
      Notes & Numbers   244

★. Dream Parties:
    Themes, Schemes and Dreams   245

30. Planning Sheets: Worksheets, Play Sheets   253
      Postal Chart   255
      Bar Chart   260
      Master Planning Sheet   257
      Resources Worksheet   259

    Index   261

THE WONDER COMPANY, INC.

Dear Readers:

Patty Sachs is well qualified to assume the title of 'idea queen of the United States of America'. Her inexhaustible treasure trove of special events ideas has produced many of the finest events in our nation's history. Patty realizes that today's special events planners and producers must constantly reinvent the profession by creating new, sparkling ideas that will attract and captivate guests. Patty is an expert in this regard and has written a compendium of ideas that will stimulate the thinking of many new and experienced special events planners. You will be inspired and enthused as you read this book to create bigger and better events under the tutelage of a great professional-Patty Sachs.

Thanks,

Joe Jeff Goldblatt
Executive Producer

Author- "Special Event's: The Art and Science of Celebration"; a Van Nostrand Reinhold, book.

2600 Virginia Avenue N.W. Suite 1100 Washington, D.C. 20037 (202) 337-2600 FAX (202) 337-1885

'Thanks a Million'
SYNDICATED COLUMN

PERCY ROSS

Dear Readers:

A CREATIVE THINKER WHO PLANS A PARTY WITH AS MUCH
SUCCESS AS PATTY SACHS, SHOULD BE EXALTED AS PARTY
QUEEN OF NOT ONLY THIS CENTURY, BUT THE NEXT ONE,
AND THE ONE AFTER THAT!

Your friend,

Percy Ross

5151 EDINA INDUSTRIAL BLVD.   MINNEAPOLIS, MN. 55435   (612) 835-2400

HENNY YOUNGMAN
KING OF THE ONE LINERS

Aug 25, 90

Hello Patty

First, nice to hear from you "weddings Parties and Celebrations in Book form, great idea: We all need a book like this. Your ideas in the past have always been important to me. You know how to complete things, which is so important.

As you know I'm always available for these type functions. Good luck

Henny (himself)

P.S. Call me and we'll dine at the Friars Club

77 west 55th st.   new york 19, n.y.   phone (212) 581-7755

Laughable Laws

☺   In San Francisco there's an ordinance banning picking up used confetti to throw again.

☺   It is a criminal offense in Massachusetts to wear a costume while collecting a bad debt.

☺   Forbidden in Belt, Montana, are: the Tango, the Duck Wobble, the Angle Worm Wiggle and the Kangaroo Glide.

☺   New Hampshire law forbids you to tap your foot, nod your head, or in any way keep time to music in a tavern, restaurant or cafe.

☺   It is against the law in Oklahoma to get a fish drunk.

☺   Under Alabama law, the wearer of a false moustache who causes unseemly laughter in church is liable to arrest.

☺   A Chicago law forbids eating in a place that is on fire.

☺   San Francisco prohibits elephants from strolling down Market Street unless they are on a leash.

(How do they expect us to have fun, anyway...?)

THE CAKE CONCEPT

The cake, with all of its unique shapes, flavors, fillings, trimmings and presentations will top off any celebration. When was the last time that you attended a special occasion where there wasn't cake??? Some folks think that if there's no cake it is not a "real" special occasion.

The cakes you may have seen have conveyed wishes for:

    Happy Birthday
    Happy Anniversary
    Happy New Baby
    Happy New Home
    Happy Wedding Day
    Happy Bar/Bat Mitzvah
    Happy Housewarming

Happy New Pool
Happy New Grandparents
Happy New Car
Happy Valentines Day
Happy New Year
Happy Fourth of July
Happy Labor Day
Happy Bastille Day
Happy Halloween
Happy Confirmation
Happy Easter
Happy St. Patrick's Day
Congratulations on Your Retirement
Congratulations on Your Graduation
Congratulations on Your New Job
Congratulations on Your Promotion
Congratulations on Your Engagement
Congratulations Tournament Champs
Congratulations Licensed Driver
Congratulations on being Single
Good Luck Team
Good Luck In College
Bon Voyage
Have Fun At Camp
Have a Great Trip
Welcome Home
Thank You, Staff
Merry Christmas
Welcome Class of '__
Welcome, _____ Family Reunion

And the hundreds of other messages on those cakes
that are baked, decorated and devoured every day,
in every state, city and province.

You may be thinking, "What is all of this 'cakeology' leading to, anyway"?

Well, it is my attempt to get you into a mood, frame of mind, attitude, perspective, or ,if you will, philosophy, for reading this book. It is a simplified analogous approach to planning weddings, parties, and celebrations that will be successful in accomplishing your specific goals.

A special event is divided into three parts:

the planning and anticipation, the event itself and finally, the memory. A truly successful event includes an even balance of all three experiences.

An event, which is held either for personal or for business reasons can be viewed as a cake.

✳ The unique ingredients make up the flavor or the overall purpose of the reasons for celebrating.

✳ The baker aided by the dependability and quality of the oven represents the planning and implementation of the event.

✳ The uniqueness and surprise is in the filling and shape, which could be likened to the theme and how it's carried out. This facet would include decorations, music, entertainment and gifts/favors.

✳ Then, the adornments and decorations (frosting, flowers, special trimmings, candles, figures, lettering and special drawings) are what make the event beautiful, personal, sensory and memorable. These elements are the presentations, tributes, roasts and toasts.

* The pan and utensils represent the location or site of the event, along with the equipment, food, beverage and service.

When you present your *"cake"* I know it will cause excitement and admiration. Your guests will anticipate and savor it, taste it, find it delicious and in many cases, they'll even take some home to enjoy later (why, I've known folks to put cake under their pillow for good luck.)

This book will, through hundreds of plans and ideas (recipes) help you to create batters, layers, tiers, fillings, flavors, frostings, decorations, and trimmings to produce cakes to fulfill all of your themes, schemes, and dreams.

~*Chapter*~

The Event

WHAT MAKES IT SPECIAL?

The elements of an event are the people, decor, entertainment, activities and finally, the food and beverage.

People: Rated 1-10

The way people dress and the things they say, reflect the amount of enthusiasm and zest with which they approach life. The person who shows up at a costume party wearing a pair of sunglasses is a sharp contrast to the "masquerade maniac" who comes dressed as a "Trekkie," pointed ears, antennae and all.

Decorations: Rated 1-10

A table decoration can be a bud vase of daisies with two votive candles or it can be a brightly colored popcorn ball, with cotton candy on sticks puffing out in all directions, all dramatically displayed on a toy drum that is rotating. Room decor can be a few small bunches of colored balloons or a 100-foot tall logo constructed of balloons and mylar. Banners, balloons, signs, lights, props, plants, flowers and candles in the right combinations create surroundings that make an event special.

Food and Beverage: Rated 1-10.

You can sit down to a meal (simple fare, served on a plain white cloth, on white china) or you can sit down to an experience (gourmet menu, set on pastel pink cloth and served on white china with a silver rim.) Colors, textures, flavors, and temperatures of food and beverage make the difference in just eating or experiencing. The way the food is presented, the table settings, the linens, glassware, serving pieces, ice sculptures, flowers and decorations, candles or special lighting are all factors in the final experience.

Music and Entertainment: Rated 1-10

Music can blend in and create a backdrop of sound or it can overwhelm and interfere with your enjoyment of the other guests. If properly planned, music can ignite and excite, it can raise spirits or merely blend into the background. The right type of music played at the right time and volume help make an event outstanding. Entertainment presentations can be generic in content such as magic, comedy or singing that is directed to the general public or it can be designed using information, jargon, names and incidents that are specifically for your group

Activities: Rated 1-10

The ultimate object in planning activities is to involve your guests at their own comfort level. Mandatory participation of any kind is not a good idea. Only in very rare cases will an activity work with the entire group. Organize contests, lessons, participation activities that can be enjoyed by the "I'm game" type as well as the "I'll just sit here and watch" type and everyone in between.. Acting like a kid, working up a competitive sweat, showing off talents, skills and creative flairs are all good ways of guest involvement. The non-participants can be the audience and the judges. Guest's involvement at their own level will make an event memorable for them.

The energy and appeal of the various event components will establish their rating, hopefully from 7-10. Any event element of this rating will stand out and be noticed. One by one, carefully select and polish those facets that will create the excitement and the sparkle that does, indeed, make an event special.

As you make the ultimate plans for your occasion use this guideline to direct and elevate each of the main ingredients aiming for a perfect 10, of course.

In order to make guests feel important you need to do things that let them know that you joyfully anticipated their being at your event. Yes, it's good to see a great and big turnout . . . but remember that you can give your guests the feeling that the party wouldn't have been the same without them...that they would have been missed and that their not being present would have lessened the excellence of the event. Giving them the pleasant awareness that *"Our hosts went all out for us"* is all that it takes to accomplish this mission.

Recap: "Specialness" can be a look, a sound, a taste, a smell, a touch, or an emotion. As a guest it can be found in something you do, or that is done to or for you. For some, the memory of an event may be special because it made them laugh . . . others relish shedding tears. A theme will always create a special attitude and mood. But even the most elaborate and extravagant theme will fade in one's mind if there wasn't a connection or involvement on a personal level. There must always be something that nourishes the sensory, that subliminally suggests that your guest was a "guest of honor."

~Chapter~

2

Special People

MAKE EVENTS SPECIAL

Each of us knows a person who brings festivity and celebration to every day of life; a person who takes the opportunity to rejoice and pay tribute to the most simple and everyday occurrences. This person usually loves life and people and celebrates the accomplishments of others as his own. This is the sort of person who will talk to strangers on airplanes, gather business cards, exchange numbers and addresses, recommend books and resources, and will network anything. Truly a special being.

If you are the person that I have just described, chances are that you already know how to throw a heckuva party. In the process of enjoying and studying people, you probably have collected ideas, clippings, brochures and samples. You probably love trade shows even if they don't relate to your field of employment or interest. When it's time for you to participate in the planning of an event for your private or work life, you are loaded with ideas and resources. Others probably seek you out and pick your brain for help in their planning. You are not the person for whom this book has been written. However, you will probably enjoy it the most!!

This book, an eclectic collection of ideas, how-to's and resources, is for the vast majority of you who recognize and appreciate a truly wonderful party or celebration, but when it comes to giving one of your own, you panic.

The good news is that this book can serve as a safety net for your "high wire" act—planning and giving a party for your friends, family or business associates.

Most folks are either completely or partially responsible for putting together at least one big "do" in their lives, and it is usually a wedding, anniversary or reunion. When this ultimate challenge first comes along there may be some offers of help from a committee, team, siblings, kids or fellow employees. Sad to say, eventually you may wind up on your own unless you can effectively supervise your helpers and confidently delegate responsibility.

In this book you will find formulas, tips, schedules, estimates and warnings that you can use to compensate for disappearing volunteers. By using some of my bits of advice and following the counsel of friends or family members who have planned a similar event, you can stage your own hit show..

For the experienced planner who is familiar with basic formulas, schedules, and resources this book will still hold a wealth of ideas to help in brainstorming and getting those creative juices flowing. It holds information that will prove invaluable when putting on an original and one-of-a-kind knockout event.

Most of the ideas have been tried and retried and need only be slightly altered to fit your theme. You will also find some wild and wacky musings that should definitely be put into action (according to this expert) and are almost guaranteed to succeed. Then there are those priceless passages that contain out-and-out "fearless fantasies" (try-at-your-own-risk) stuff, that are the ravings of a truly "pooped" party planner who has, in an attempt to become a world famous event expert, inhaled far too much helium, cut a dangerous amount of confetti squares, danced the Limbo and Hokey-Pokey a mile or two over the limit, and most obvious of all, has consumed too much leftover caviar. (Ed: My heart bleeds...)

And now, for the exciting part . . . none of the "tried and true", "strongly suggested" or famous "fearless fantasies" are marked or labeled as such. You are on your own. If you spot an idea that appeals to you, try it. These ideas, your zestful spirit and determination combined with an ability to apply the *"They'll never take us alive"* philosophy will help you succeed at meeting the challenge of successful event planning.

You, my dear reader, are undoubtedly special for many reasons and because you are reading this book, I suspect that you are about to become even more special through the planning and implementing of an important celebration. I am thrilled to be a part of that.

So, please, be my guest! Plan creatively and thoroughly, ask for help, have fun and most of all, put something special into all of your events-- something special called **"love."**

CREATING THE CAKE

We've established that a celebration can be compared to a cake, now we will illustrate how the planning of an event can be like creating a cake, layer by layer, ingredient by ingredient. Each phase of baking a cake is equally important and must be executed in a certain order with close attention to detail. This analogy not only fits perfectly, but I think it is highly appropriate since we all know that cakes are synonymous with celebrations.

Step One.

Deciding on the type of the cake: (Sheet, Layer, Tier, Fruit, Angel Food, Bundt, to name a few.)

This is generally the style of your event which includes such possibilities as Formal Dinner Party, Picnic at the Lake, Informal Open House, Costume Ball or Tailgating. The list is long and varied.

Step Two.

Selecting the shape and flavor for your cake: (White, chocolate, spice, marble, carrot, lemon, Boston Cream, banana, and many more personal favorites)

The flavor and the shape of your special event is the theme that you decide upon and since a theme is not essential, a plain white cake would represent an event that simply happens in an uncomplicated, traditional manner.

Step Three.

Planning the size of your cake.

After making a guest list, you can determine the quantity of cake that you will need to serve. This factor will give you an idea of of what kind of pan to use (the location) or how it will be served.

Step Four.

Decide upon the ingredients, the quality, the variations and the special utensils that you will need to prepare this most important delicacy.

In essence, this step would be determining the budget and the vendors. This process is vital and if creatively implemented, will not be too frustrating. This would be the step that involves selecting invitations, table linens and serving ware, the menu and all equipment that will be necessary to implement all of the details of the event. This will include all the instructions for the caterer or sales representative at the event site.

Step Five.

Combining these personally-chosen ingredients, using outstanding utensils carefully and precisely to create the basic batter. Blend gently for the required amount of time for you are nearing the baking phase. —

This is the basic plan and how it is coordinated and put into effect your final product. It is the foundation and frame of your event. After it is placed in the oven, that is, all contracted and arranged for, your celebration cake need only be checked periodically to make sure it is coming along nicely.

Step Six.

Choosing the delicious and delightful surprise fillings.

Music, entertainment, hosts and hostesses, valet parkers, special gifts or favors, and general table and room decorations, flowers, balloons and signage, are all components which make up the overall ambiance and beauty of the event. The mood or appeal of the function will be settled by all of these comfortable, atmospheric and esthetic factions.

Step Seven.

Adding frosting and trimmings for the cake make the total product good, great or greatest. Candles, icing, flowers, tiny figures, messages and customized drawings set that cake apart from any other.

Face painters, caricaturists, skits, video presentations, specialty talent such as magicians, jugglers, mimes or ventriloquists are the embellishments and extra touches which give a clear message that you have planned this celebration with verve, vitality and loads of love.

Planning Process with 3X5 Cards:

The process that works for me (coincidentally) calls for dozens of 3x5 recipe cards. By writing each and every detail on a card of its own you can keep shuffling those cards and continue to make notations of pertinent information on each. After I have made all of these cards, I categorize them according to what area of the plan they are a part of, such as: menu, decorations, entertainment, equipment, rentals, staff, and printed items. I also put them in a dated file to remind me that they need to be verified or confirmed.

The second part of this process is to make a master list of all the cards recording the name of the person to whom each has been delegated. This plan is highly effective in a situation where there is a chairperson, committees and committee members. When a card is given out it is noted on the master file. When the task has been completed its card is returned to the chairperson and used only as a back up resource.

I suggest, that after you have successfully planned and implemented an event, you keep these cards, especially the ones that have names and phone numbers, price quotes, style numbers and other valuable information. You can file them away and save them for your next event and have them available for reference requests.

The following is an illustration of a detail card

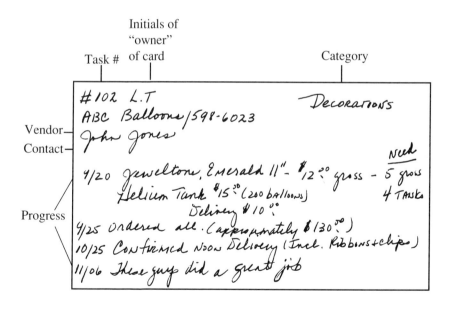

Notes & Numbers

THE COMMON BOND

The theme's the thing. Did someone say that? Well, everyone is saying it now. When people announce that they're having a party or even a wedding, one of the first questions is "What's the theme?" Setting a theme generates excitement, creates a commonality among the guests, and gives the host a plan of attack, so to speak. With a theme there is an underlying feeling, mood or motive for the event. That is, if all the guests are planning costumes, searching for a clue, or digging up an old photo, they are in sync. By the time they arrive at the event, a spirit of togetherness has already been established. First, the theme is introduced with the invitation, then emphasized and reinforced with the decoration, entertainment, food and favors.

When selecting a theme it is helpful to brainstorm with friends or family, (especially the creative types,) for ideas, if you can. If the party is for an individual or couple, begin by considering the following: hobbies, talents, occupations, quirks, interests, dreams and goals.

Example: Birthday, a la Garbage

After I'd spent a few minutes chatting with a client we established that her husband was most famous for being very neat and sometimes "prematurely" tidy. He was known as the "host-most-likely" to pull out a big garbage bag and start "after party" cleaning up...before the party was over. When his guests first witnessed this behavior, they took offense, but when they realized that he was just doing "his thing," they started teasing him about it and expecting it. Well, we took off on this garbage bag idea and when we finished, the invitation was written on a little plastic litter bag, the guests were instructed to dress in trash bags, food was served in pails, buckets and baskets traditionally used for waste. (It helped that this is the age of brightly colored plastics that are pretty enough to "eat out of.") Dancing to the sounds of the *Trashmen* and giving a friendly "incineration" (a la roast) of the guest proved to be "throw-away" entertainment. The highlight of the evening's festivities was a special surprise for the guest of honor: At about 10 p.m. all of the guests stood up and left the room. In moments they came marching back in with their trash bags and immediately started cleaning up. Now, that's an example of taking a small detail of a person's life and blowing it up to a full-fledged theme. It is all in good (and, in this case, "clean") fun, and hopefully, in good taste.

Weddings with themes are very popular these days. You need not go to the extent of skydiving, mountain climbing, or hang gliding as seen on the news. But lovely themes can be adopted.

These are just scant theme descriptions and suggestions to give you a start.

> **A Luau:** Hawaiian or island theme, palm trees, leis, etc.
>
> **Christmas in July:** (The bride's favorite time of year was Christmas, but the wedding took place in mid-summer.)
>
> **Victorian:** In an old mansion, chamber music, costumed servers.
>
> **Italian:** Red, white and green decor, a pasta bar, accordion music, gondola rides (if you're near water) and vino.

Mexican Fiesta: Authentic food, mariachi music, crisp, white lace and huge paper flowers for decorations.

Renaissance: Jousters, mimes and jugglers, Ye Olde style food, (turkey legs, fruit) hammer dulcimer and harp music.

Cruise Ship: The Love Boat, lavish buffets (don't forget the ice sculpture,) typical ship activities such as shuffleboard, lounge acts, gambling, bon voyage signs and streamers.

Gatsby: Pastel and pretty, big band or orchestra music, cool and fancy food and drink, fresh flowers and mirrors to decorate.

Mardi Gras: Elaborate and elegant masks as part of the decor and for the guests, costumed servers, grand and gala music for dancing., Cajun food.

Skiing in the Alps: Swiss fondue food service, Alpine music, mountain decor and "Swiss banks" as favors, yodelers and Tyroleon characters.

Broadway Shows: Whatever the show: *My Fair Lady*, *Oklahoma*, *Hair*, *Cats*, take off on the theme.

Same Color Themes: Everyone wears a certain color, the food is all served in that color, the decor is that color. For weddings it is usually pastel. They are gorgeous.

Eras: Twenties, Forties, Fifties, Sixties and Seventies are all popular. The clothing, food, music and games of the era make a great theme reception.

Holidays: Halloween, Valentines Day, Fourth of July, Thanksgiving, Christmas or New Years

Hobbies or Occupations: Sports, music, art, cooking, fashion, automobiles, books, travel, Lawyers, doctors, computer industry, retail, trades, entertainment and business. When the couple have a mutual occupation this theme idea can be a lot of fun and a creative challenge. It is also possible to combine two careers such as Law and Music, Medicine and Travel, etc.

A couple that I knew were both actors. For their reception they took everyone to a production of *"I Do, I Do,"* at the local dinner theater. Another theatrical thing that this couple did was to have a *"show"-er.* Everyone had to perform a skit, song, or reading on stage—since it did take place in a Little Theater.

Surrounding a traditional ceremony, the theme can add beauty, enchantment and fun. Again, the theme pulls the guests together in an even closer way.

A very clever lady put together a great surprise Safari for her husband's birthday party. His dream was to go on a great elephant hunt, so she took off on that fact. She turned the country club into a jungle, told the guests to dress in their pith helmets and khakis, loaded the band with jungle drums and dressed the wait staff in native attire. A crazy invitation was written on a big green leaf (crepe paper) using lots of "jungle-eze." The collection of characters in attendance was made complete by the arrival of an awesome and authentic witch doctor. The gift/favor was a photo taken with the "Doc" and framed in mock bamboo. This party was, to say the least, really "wild." The decorations were comprised of bamboo, palm leaves, coconuts, gorilla masks, voodoo dolls. The *"love potion #9"* was dispensed from a big black kettle.

Sometimes the theme is as simple as a color scheme. Black and white weddings are popular and very dramatic. Ice cream socialscall for pastel and pretty tints; F. Scott Fitzgerald and "Gatsby" parties encourage those frothy white gowns and crisp linen suits; some "over-the-hill" celebrations instruct the guests to dress as mourners. When you put a special theme dress code on your invitation, it means that your guests are part of both the decor and the entertainment.

Gimmicks can set a theme, and although they may seem silly to some, they do provide the "path" of planning.

✱ Dressing as a look-alike to the guest of honor brings out the "kindness or cruelty" in people. Photo masks are perfect for this theme. (PLANNING RESOURCES: Chapter 29, Masks).

✱ A Non-Party theme had the guests arriving to find nary a sign of a party. After forming teams, the guests went out in search of an assigned component of the party, i.e., decorations, music, food and beverage, etc. When they returned, they put the ingredients together and lo, and behold, they had created a co-op party.

You'll find dozens of fun and unique themes in THEME IDEAS, Chapter 5.

Themes, schemes and dreams will add to the festivity and continuity of your events as they provide you with a "road map" to follow as well as make your planning easier, more exciting and a lot more fun.

~*Chapter*~

(A)RABIAN NIGHTS TO (Z)ORBA'S DANCE

Themed events are exciting, entertaining, involving, creative, fun-filled and memorable. There are as many potential themes as there are events. When you consider that a theme can be as simple as everyone wearing the same color, you can imagine the myriad possibilities. I have gone from A to Z and listed just some of the theme ideas. It will give you a good start and your creative powers can move you to even more great ideas.

Themes, A to Z

A

Artists and Models, Aerobics Action, Academy Awards, Animal Crackers, American Bandstand, Abracadabra, Alphabet Soup, Alice in Wonderland, A.B.C's, Arabian Nights.

B

Baby Days, Baseball, Breakfast at Tiffany's, Boy meets Girl, Big Top, Black and White, Bargain Basement, Beach Blanket Bingo, Brazilian, Bowling, Blazing Saddles, Beer Tasting.

C

Chef/Cooking, California Dreamin', Chorus Line, Chinatown, Caveman, Cruise Ship, Cookie Monsters, CLUE Game, Couch Potatoes, Comedy Club, Circus, Carnival, Clowning Around.

D

Disneyland, Dolly Parton, Desert Island, Dance Fever, Diamond Jim's, Dogpatch Days, Detective, Dick Tracy.

E

Entertainment Tonight, Elvis Lives, Election Night, Egyptian Nights, Education, Electronics.

F

Football Fantasy, Favorite (anything), Food, French, Fashion, Funny Papers, Flying High, Farm, Flintstones, Fur and Feather, Filmland, Fall Fling, Forties, Fifties.

G

Glamour, Glitter and Glitz, Greek, Gatsby, Garden Party, Green Acres, Game Shows, Gold Rush Days, Guys & Dolls, Golf Tourney.

H

Health Nuts, Humor, Hollywood, Horror Movies, Happy Days, Hats off to.., Hawaiian, Hoedown, Heroes, Hillstreet Blues, Hobbies, Horsing Around.

I

Inventions and Innovations, Indian (American and eastern) Italian, Irish, IQ Tests, Ice Cream Social, Ice Skating.

J

Jungle-out-there, Jazz Junction, Junkyard Dogs, Japanese, Jack-of-all-trades, Judge and Jury.

K

King Kong, Klondike Days, Kids' Day, Kindergarten, Kite Flying.

L

Literary Lovers, Las Vegas, Laurel & Hardy, Latin America, Leap Year, Lumberjack Days, L.A. Law, Luau, Lords and Ladies (leaping or not.)

M

Music Video Night, Movie Mania, Mexican Fiesta, Monte Carlo, Mission Impossible, Medieval, Medicine, Manhattan, Magic, Military, M.A.S.H., Mystery Party, Martians, Moonwalk, Ma & Pa Kettle.

N

Neptune, Nightclubs, Nautical, Nerds, New York, Night Court.

O

Opera (soap or Night-At-The) Opryland, Old Times, Old Fashioned, Occult, Oriental, Occupations, Oakies.

P

Polka Fest, Pizza and Pasta, Paris, Pajama, Partners in Crime, Pig Roast, Picnic in the Park, Pirates, Princes and Princesses, Practical Jokers, Premier Party, Punk Rockers.

Q

Quotes(famous), Quiz Kids, Queens & Kings.

R

Rodeo, Ranch life, Rock and Roll, Riverboat, Ragtime, Radio Days, Renaissance, Roman, Roller-skating, Romance, Royalty, Russia, Running, Rapping, Rich & Famous, Rocky Horror.

S

Square Dance, Space Ship, Stars and Stripes, Star Search, Sleighride, Show Biz, Seasons, School Days, Saturday Night Live, Sailing, Self-Help, Secret Desires, Sit-Coms, Single Life, Skiing, Skating, Super Sleuth, South Pacific, Speakeasy, Sports, Supernatural, Space Travel, Switzerland, Sixties, Seventies, Sesame Street, St. Valentines Day Massacre, Scavenger Hunt.

T

Time Warp, Tea Dance, Toyland, Television, Twenties, Thirties, Tinseltown, Twilight Zone, Travel, Treasure Hunt, Transylvania, Theater Party, Tax Day, Tasteless, Tailgate, Teenager, Talent Nite, Tacky, Tyroleon, Twins.

U

Ugly, Underworld, Unemployed, Underwear, Uniforms, Untouchables, Uppercrust, U.S.A., Urban Cowboys.

V

Victory, Victorian, Voting Day, Videos, Vogue, Vintage, Valley Kids, Vagabonds.

W

Wartimes, Winners, White on White, Winter Wonderland, Wagon Train, Wizard of Oz, Wine Tasting, Washington, D.C.

X

Xercize [Ed:Excuse me???]

Y

Yokels, Younger Days, Yo Yos, Yakety Yak, Yellow Days, Yesterday Again, Yuppies, Yuletide, Yearbooks.

Z

Zoo Parade, Zap Games, Zodiac

Whew! That is a lot of partying. And to think that there are a lot more in the creative recesses of your minds! These suggestions are just to jiggle your juices. Once you set your theme, go for the gusto and be a "Theme-maniac." It's the reason to have a theme.

Some of my favorite theme party ideas: (lately)

Adventure Club (ongoing theme group): Twelve couples join together to make up this exciting and growth-oriented monthly meeting group. Each month one of the couples, in turn, is responsible for planning a day or evening that is filled with adventure, new ideas and experiences. The experiences can consist of places, activities, meeting an interesting and vital person, trying to do new things or participating as a spectator at a new event. The group is usually formed by four couples, each of which selects two unknown-to-the-others couples. Thus, the first adventure is meeting several new people. Tastings, demonstrations, lessons, competitions, excursions and encounters are all viable parts of an adventure gathering. Videotape documentation of these evenings provides a once-a-year recap of the club's activities. Each couple pays their own way, cannot miss a month without a serious reason and is responsible for planning one adventure gathering a year. What a way to grow!

Limousine Scavenger Hunts: Couples or singles can spend an evening in high excitement racing around town collecting miscellaneous and mostly remote items to win a prize never intended to motivate anyone to win. The competition is steep and the action cut-throat at times. If you do not win fair and square, you get drummed out of the game. For starters the contestants meet for cocktails and hors d'oeuvre to get acquainted with each other, collect their hunt list and rules. After the hunt the scavengers return to the original point for the prize presentation and more socializing and dancing.

Mate Hunting Theme Parties: This plan has several variations that will work. The concept is for a group of single men or women to organize a theme party for eligible (preferably, wanting to become ineligible) persons to meet, socialize and hopefully "hook up". Each host/hostess invites a number of others who are in turn, instructed to bring someone of the opposite sex that they would heartily recommend for a potential date. (Some have called this party Platonic Potluck.) After a series of these parties the principle planners found husbands, so it does work. The key is to have a sophisticated, well planned theme complete with nice invitations, good food and decor, and a quality guest list.

Note: Costume parties probably won't work unless the group has met several times. Happy Hunting and be sure and invite me! [Ed: What do you think this is, the Personals?] (You never know!)

~Chapter~

6

The Schedule

THE MINUTE-BY-MINUTE WALTZ

As a host, how many times have you reached the end of an event and realized that you have forgotten a very important detail? Something costly in time, money and energy was wasted because that detail was forgotten in the hustle and bustle. (Just like Louis Anderson's mom, who always forgets the sweet potatoes at Thanksgiving.)

During the excitement and action of a gala party, it's easy to forget something unless you have a tight schedule, which you follow to a T, which lists every detail and duty.

Key Scheduling Points:

After you have made an overview list of all activities you want to include in the event, create a minute-by-minute timetable. Estimate the duration of each event, then add it all up to make sure you are not over or under the total amount of time you have allotted for the party.

✳ Verbally, walk through the event to establish the flow of each activity in the schedule.

✳ On the day of the event keep this schedule with you and stick to it as closely as you can.

✳ If you follow your schedule strictly, you'll feel more in control and a nice flow will be created.

✳ One thing to remember is that people often arrive late and leave early, so major presentations should be made at the peak time. Guests should be told when these will occur so that they can be on hand for them.

✳ Without acting like a camp counselor (no clip boards or whistles, please), you will direct the production and subtly move from activity to activity.

An example of an event timetable:

Fiftieth Anniversary Party for the Smiths .

6:00 - 6:30	Guests arrive and receive name tags and seating assignment..
6:00 - 7:00	Cocktails and hors d'oeuvres Piano Player (in foyer)
7:00 - 8:00	Dinner and wine Trio (in dining room)
8:00 - 8:15	Dessert and champagne Trio & singer (in dining room)
8:00 - 8:30	Entertainment lines up and ballots are passed to guests
8:30 - 9:30	Show, voting, gifts passed to guests, coffee served. Full band
9:30 - 9:40	Song sheets passed (get volunteers from audience) Note: Turn lights up
9:40 - 10:00	Song and toasts from guests (Use band's tape deck) Note: Turn lights down
10:00 - 11:00	Dancing and socializing Full band

11:00 - 11:15	Dance contests Full band and Emcee Note: Turn lights up
11:15 - 11:30	Prizes, thanks, announcements Mom and Dad speech
11:30 - 12:00	Dancing. Guests will start to say goodnight

Note: The lights are left up after the speeches to give the idea that it is about time for the event to end.

As you can see, each minute is accounted for and the food and entertainment are coordinated so that something is always going on. There are no dead spots.

The key to the success of using this schedule is to give a copy of it to the caterer, the band leader and the room manager.

If yours is an open house event, the schedule may only serve as a check list for certain aspects of the event, such as the food and beverage inspection, guest book placement, photos, etc. It will serve as a reminder to "make rounds," seeing to it that everyone has what they need, and that things are going as planned.

If you are planning an event that has a wide variety of activities, the job of schedule keeper is a major one and should be assigned during the early planning stages. The person who has this assignment should be familiar with the house, the space, what equipment is available and where to find things. If the schedule keeper has to interrupt the host from time to time with questions, it defeats the purpose of having one.

War story:

The hostess had planned a lovely gift for all of the guests, to be placed in their cars while they were partying. Somehow, the beautifully wrapped packages were found the morning after in a carton, in the garage.

Another war story:

The host had gone to great lengths to have napkins imprinted with the guest of honor's silhouette. The beautiful works of art were found in a carton during the cleanup. (Unlike left-over chili, they weren't better the next day.) A schedule keeper with a checklist would have prevented these oversights.

For highly-structured events a program is given to each guest to make it easier for them to follow the schedule of entertainment and activities. The hosts can delegate the following of the printed schedule, which is augmented with a detailed list of duties, to a non-guest (perhaps a member of the Party Pool). This leaves the party-givers free to enjoy their guests while the party is kept running smoothly by the coordinator.

~*Chapter*~

7

The Space

LET'S *NOT* BUILD A BARN

If you are lucky enough to have a home or work place that is suitable for entertaining, you can throw a party exactly the way you like. Over the years, you may have accumulated the equipment or supplies that are necessary for celebrating any occasion. However, this chapter is written for those who will need to create an event in a rented or borrowed space. It will outline the ideal situation and help you choose an event location that is right for the size and type of function that you are planning. At the end of this chapter I will address some of the problems that arise when the space you are forced to use is less than perfect.

The options for special event locations are varied and range from hotel ballrooms or meeting facilities with accommodations and food and beverage for overnight guests to the party room of an apartment complex where you provide most everything yourself. Between those two choices are private halls and houses where the hosts can arrange for food and beverage service; parks, gardens, terraces or courtyards; private banquet rooms at favorite restaurants, and unique sites such as mansions, museums, warehouses, ranches, country clubs, farms and even the zoo. (See UNIQUE SITES, Chapter 8)

Before you embark upon the search for a site, think back over the past year or so and make mental note of any places you've been that may be appropriate for your event. Keep in mind that your unique set of circumstances, i.e., your theme, the number of guests, your budget and the activities planned, must all be considered. When you have made a prospective site list, call to determine key factors: cost, capacity, limitations and most important, availability. Then set up viewing meetings with sales or catering managers.

It is usually time/cost effective if one person visits the possible options, narrows these down to the best choices, and returns with other principal decision makers to meet and finalize the decision.

Planning Events in Less Than Perfect Spaces

Challenge: Small group in large space

❋ Create dividers with folding screens, tall plants, plants standing on pedestals, bouquets of balloons on pedestals, props or backdrops, hanging banners of inexpensive fabric, trellis or plywood facades.

❋ Place dividers at angles in corners of the room to give the room new walls and diminish the space. Use round tables placed close to each other rather than spread out over the room.

❋ If you have buffet tables, bring them out into the room instead of against the wall.

❋ Again, create a backdrop for the buffet serving area.

❋ Drape inexpensive fabric from the ceiling, corner to corner, to create the effect of a lower ceiling.

❋ Use low lighting, lots of candles and bunches of balloons that float above the tables as part of the centerpieces.

❋ Anderson's catalog is filled with lovely, fantasy-land props and effects that will help to fill some of the excess space. (See RESOURCES, Chapter 29).

✳ If you have a dance floor, keep it small and intimate, too. Place small cafe style tables around it to fill space and provide extra seating.

Challenge: Large group in small space

✳ Remove most of the furniture and provide small tables for seating.

✳ Serve buffet style with several stations so that guests can get to food easily. Passing food will also make serving more convenient.

✳ If you can use extra space such as a patio or balcony, rent a canopy to make it weatherproof.

✳ To avoid setting up extra tables, use every flat surface for food. (Pianos, desks, shelves, ledges.)

✳ A great new rental table is bar height and round. It accommodates guests in a standing-room-only situation.

✳ To provide additional seating for children, bring in picnic tables and make a special festive area for the little ones.

✳ If you are serving a seated meal, use long banquet tables.

Challenge: Casual atmosphere, formal occasion

* Use white cloth tablecloths and napkins, mylar or mirror accessories, candles and lots of greens.

* There are chair covers that make even folding chairs look dressed up. (See RESOURCES, Chapter 29)

* Twinkle lights on a string, candelabra, and colored spotlights will create an elegant atmosphere.

* If a room has an unattractive floor, you can camouflage it with a piece of rented carpeting.

* When intertwined, clear balloons with lights inside make a sophisticated and elegant decoration staple.

* If the room is bare and unattractive, rent paintings and prints from the library and/or drape fabric over doors, windows and walls to dress it up. (See ECONOMY EVENTS, Chapter 20)

Challenge: Formal decor, casual event

* If it doesn't cause too much of a clash, use checkered tablecloths or colored cloths with streamers and ribbons to create a picnic feeling.

* Add baskets, craft paper, straw flowers, country props and casual backdrops.

＊ Serve food in buckets, tins and use paper products.

＊ Props such as park benches, hay and straw bales, wood fence sections, crates, street lamps, gazebos and trees or plants will create a comfortable and homey atmosphere.

＊ Balloons and banners can be casual and yet festive if mixed with homespun natural fabrics, paper and gauze.

Special Event Site Information

Fun in Frisco:

Imagine piling your group of (35 seated, 15 standees) guests onto an authentic San Francisco cable car for a hillside party or reception. Serve a plate of Rice-a-roni, a slice of sourdough bread and import some lovely vino from Napa Valley. And I suppose, to make it perfect, you could invite Tony Bennet to sing "you-know-what." (I'll come if you invite me.) The reservation number is 415-922-2425 (that's for the cable car, not for me!)

41

Special people, doing special things:

Days Inn of America has instituted a plan whereby they are providing temporary lodging and employment for homeless people who are referred by various agencies. When you shop around for your event space, give Days Inn special consideration as a salute for their generous efforts to make a difference in today's world. If their banquet space will work for you, by booking there, you give Days Inn a helping hand to give the homeless a helping hand. For more information about the program you can contact your local Days Inn.

Good luck on your search for a perfect location for your function. Be flexible, take some time and the perfect spot will develop. It may be right in your own back yard!

Notes & Numbers

~Chapter~

8
Unique Sites

(A)TRIUM TO (Z)OO

One of the secrets of success in party planning is in choosing the location. If you want to add measurably to the turnout at your event, hold it in a space that is new, popular or unusual. You will appeal to the human characteristics of curiosity and adventurousness.

Almost everyone has been to a soiree in a banquet hall or ballroom that was elaborately decorated to look very elegant but it still did not stir the senses. Somehow it was cold, too stiff or too formal. It just didn't feel friendly! This chapter will suggest some innovative venues and ways that can be utilized to match a theme, mood or personality of an event.

How to make the choice: As I have mentioned, the first thing to remember is that the space should fit the event. Holding your function in a unique space that has a similar or compatible atmosphere to your theme and your planned activities will save you lots of work. By not having to camouflage, dress up/down, add or remove furniture or equipment, cosmetize or disguise your space...you'll save time and cash.

Begin the hunt by calling upon a commercial photographer, film maker or model agency. These people will have the names of locations that are available for photo/filming shoots. If your event is legitimate and run by responsible adults, you might be able to convince one of these site managers or owners to let you put your event there. (Most likely for a fee.)

Warehouse

These have huge, high, open and rough space that can be adapted to almost any theme. This is a good idea when you want to be outdoors but the weather can't be depended upon to cooperate with you. In an empty warehouse you can create an island, casino, barn, haunted house, spaceship, carnival, concert hall, forest, desert, cruise ship, Olympic field, department store, sandy beach or fairyland. It is possible to bring in cars, wagons, huts, tents, bleachers, or large equipment for any demonstration or activity for fund raisers, mini-trade shows, big crowds and expansive activity.

Barn or Farm

This is an obvious choice for western or country themes, but, you can also creatively, use them for a Southwestern desert party, Renaissance Festival, First Christmas, antique car show, or vintage clothing show. The addition of outdoor activities such as horseback riding, hay and sleigh rides, rodeo antics and jousting or jesting will broaden your scope of possibility. So, you get the space, which is unique, and the benefits of being outdoors.

Public Places Museums and Zoos

These public places give your event prestige and credibility and have the built-in attraction of "party animals" or in the case of a museum or gallery, colorful and classic art on display. These spaces are designed to handle crowds that pass through, but are fine for those like yours that will stay and celebrate.

The zoo lends itself perfectly to Safari, Jungle, Tropical Island, Noah's Ark, Horticulture, Wildlife, Paradise and (with the addition of a vine to swing from) Tarzan, themes.

Museum-type themes such as Space Odyssey, Star Wars, Future Shock, Trip to the Stars, Rockin' Rockets, Space Race, Destination: Discovery, Robotic Romance, Moon Marriage would all be futuristic and exciting.

Mansions or Renovated Victorian Houses

Romance abounds in the halls of these wonderful classics where weddings, receptions, balls and galas find a perfect setting. The little nooks and crannies of a big old house provide the planner of the highly popular mystery party with the perfect hiding places for the clues, caches or corpses.

A high tea, vintage fashion showing, Victorian wedding, anniversary or centennial fete, new product introduction or a ghostly gala all fit into the surroundings of antique sprawling stairways, brocade and velvet backdrops that grace these historical atmospheres. Gambling casino parties (shades of Monte Carlo) are also right at home in the stately mansions or estates.

Office Building Atriums

You'll get the feeling that you are in a lush greenhouse, park or garden court with the trees, benches, special lighting and in some cases, waterfalls or fountains. During the day these spaces are bustling with traffic of the office tenants and their clients. But after office hours, some are available for special events. If you are interested, call the leasing office. You may have to do some fancy footwork to get an O.K., but the effort is worth it because they are excellent locations for garden-type weddings, receptions, ice cream socials, picnics in the park, family reunions, band concerts, bazaars and art/fashion events.

More Unique Places to Party:

Airplane Hangars   Car Dealerships

Shopping Malls   Movie Theaters

47

Churches and Schools	Universities
Dance Schools	Senior High Rises
Bowling Alleys	Parks and Preserves
Factories or Plants	Bed and Breakfast Inns
Amusement Parks	Racetracks
Sports Arenas	Roof Top Gardens

Parties on the Move

For hosts who are "shakers and movers", some feasible places to celebrate are on a boat, train, bus, van, R.V., plane, flat bed, or floating around the city in a hot air balloon. Limited space, restricted activity and slight discomfort are the down side of this type of entertaining, but the adventure makes up for it.

Boats & Yachts

Boats from yachts to large paddle wheelers are ideal places to party. Sunset cruises can be romantic and relaxing for a wedding reception, anniversary party or an employee event right after work. Food and beverage, music and entertainment, decorations and favors can all be presented just as in a "terra firma" location. Guests do have to make a time commitment, though, since the boat will not rush back to drop someone off. You are pretty much on for the duration. The expense of chartering a boat is definitely worth it if you are trying to entertain your guests in a luxurious and memorable way.

Boat Themes

Themes for boat celebrations are: Riverboat Ramblin', Showboat, South Pacific, Nautical, Mystery on the Mississippi (or whatever body of water you are near. Cruising or Love Boat, Island Theme (take your guests out to an island and serve the meal there.) Gilligan's Island, and lots more that you will think of.

Trains

Trains are yet another site for events. The only thing prohibiting is that your guests will be spread out and never all in one place. If you are doing a train dinner party, have an early cocktail party for everyone either in your home or on the bus. You can also bring them all together for dessert in the same way, either in your home (or event site) or on the bus. One other way to vary train parties is to move the guests from table to table as a new course is being served. It is a little hectic, and a lot of fun. Each guest is given a seating card and at the sound of the bell (or train whistle) they move to their assigned seat.

Train Party Themes

Murder on the Orient Express, Mystery Train, Soul Train,(Motown) Take the A Train (forties), Hobo Party, Freight Train, King of the Road, Monopoly Trains, Famous Train Robbery (1800's) Political Campaign Trains, Working on the Railroad.

Your guests can dress in costume, you will, of course, be the engineer or conductor. Decorations can be the old fashioned railroad lanterns, cross ties and train schedules. Toy trains, engineers striped hats, bandannas, gloves and travel brochures combined with balloons and flowers would make up unique centerpieces.

Precautions for Offbeat Sites

Certain themes will allow for and actually call for a little "roughing it:" but everything possible for the adequate comfort, safety and convenience must be provided. When holding an event in a space not normally used for special events, all of the amenities must be in place such as:

Adequate restrooms

Heat and air conditioning

Elevator (if it's a "penthouse")

Electrical for ovens and coolers

Running water, near serving areas preferred

Proper lighting in traffic areas

Parking facility with proper lighting

Fire exits

Remember: When you are planning an outdoor event, either at your home or work place, avoid the wear and tear on your carpet and rent a "Party Potty" for restrooms. The average household plumbing will backup or overflow with excessive use in a few hours time. Be prepared and put a basket of "Tidynaps" in each satellite. (Mark the doors "Women" and "Women and Men". It works!)

Whether you are planning a wedding or a bar mitzvah, both very important yet different traditional events, I hope that you will consider the possibility of having the reception or party in a unique site. Anything goes when you take a risk and let your imagination fly. If you want to transport your guests to another place either in time or in experience one of these unusual locations will be the answer.

Notes & Numbers

Notes & Numbers

~Chapter~

9

The Budget

EXPERT RATIONALIZATIONS

The most inhibiting factor in planning a creative event is the (yuk!...) budget. Before any solid commitments can be made, the amount one can or will have to spend, must be established and, with certain flexibilities, adhered to. Start by making a list of all the items that you would "like" to have for your event, make an estimated guess (after a research call or two) of the major costs involved and then present the budget for your "dream event" to the "treasurer" (the person that is paying for it, if other than yourself) for approval.

The usual approach is to start with a definite dollar figure in mind, choosing only the items that you can afford. But here is where your brains, creativity, contacts, persuasive powers and talents can pay off. If you can save in one place and use it in another, you will most likely end up having everything on your wish list... and then some.

The challenge with budgets is to distribute your precious dollars in ways that will create the most meaningful and lasting impact upon your guests. The way that you spend your event budget dollars is truly the most crucial element of your planning. In accomplishing your goal, whether personal or commercial, certain expenditures will be important and others will not contribute greatly to your event's success.

This chapter will establish the guidelines for setting a budget and give you the reasons for spending your party dollar in the suggested most effective ratios.

For instance, The budget may be based upon 150 persons and you have $25.00 per person to cover all expenses. This is not a lavish budget, but it isn't "bargain basement" either. On the assumption that most items will be purchased (versus bartered, borrowed, etc.) the suggested distribution of funds is as follows:

Invitations (includes stamp)	$ 1.00
Food, beverage, site, equipment (does not include liquor)	$8.00
Decorations and signage	1.50
Entertainment (music, specialty)	3.00
Favors, gifts, photo	3.00
Name tags, place cards, programs	1.50

Photos/video expense		2.00
TOTAL PER PERSON		$25.00

With the assistance of friends, family, co-workers or clients you can make the dollars go further in each category, but this is the most efficient distribution of the total budget and has a basic philosophy behind it. Regardless of the reason or occasion for getting folks together, these figures usually work. (The only exception being training classes or seminars, where you can replace "entertainment" with "speakers" or "trainers" and the cost might represent a larger portion of your event dollar.) How does it work? Why spend how much for what? [Ed: I know, I can't control her]

The Budget Distribution Philosophy

Invitation: I have covered invitations extensively in Chapter 10. The basic philosophy is that the invitation sets the tone and atmosphere for the event. If you look "scrimpy" at the start, well...the expectation of things to come will be less-than-exciting. Whether creative and adventurous; formal and serious; goofy and gimmicky; or sentimental and flowery give it your very best. Keep in mind, the object is to get the "biggest bang for your buck" (an old advertising term) so be sure to include your promotional message or special greeting along with or in the body of your invitation.

Location: The location is a key factor in the successful event. The atmosphere and ambiance created by the space itself is an overwhelming factor for all types of events. Try to select the space that already fits your theme or mood and avoid increasing costs by having to create the right surroundings. An example would be to plan an outdoor, woodsy, park party in an atrium or plant-filled space. This is thoroughly covered in THE SPACE, Chapter 7.

Food and Beverage: When friends, family or business associates gather, it is not just to eat and/or drink. Instead, they are coming together to reunite, socialize, pay tribute or network. Food and beverage that is modestly priced, but beautifully and elegantly presented, is another key to a successfully budgeted event.

Decorations & Signage: Replacing elaborate and perishable table decorations with those that are more practical and perhaps, lasting will add a recycling element to that part of your budget. By tying balloons in small bunches for easy disassembling you can have another innovative way to recycle the decorations--hand them out to your guests as they leave. Some hosts have artfully arranged exquisitely wrapped take-home gifts to create a table decoration that "kills two birds" by allowing the gift expenditure to serve as part of the decor. Not only is this a clever and creative idea, it is very practical. Table decorations of everlasting silk and straw flowers and inexpensive throw-aways such as foil papers and ribbons in reusable containers, all work for these "low-cost/long-life" loanable arrangements. You can blend fresh flowers and individual green or blooming plants with some the of permanent materials to help prolong the life of the decoration.

Entertainment: Although I am a devotee of live entertainment, I frequently opt for tapes and compact discs played on a first class sound system. Atmosphere is created, the theme is aptly and authentically represented, and the budget remains intact. A band or musical group (unless they are providing a very customized performance) will be an expensive and easily forgotten facet of your gem of a party. Especially at family functions where visiting and catching up with each other is the main purpose live music may not be worth the cost.

Name tags, Programs and Place cards: Here are some small but powerful forms of recognition and honor that you can pay to your guests.

✣ When personalized with exquisite calligraphy or lettering, name tags and place cards literally shout, "We're happy to see you!" and "We've looked forward to it.!"

✣ A nicely printed program of activities will help your event run smoothly, and when combined with the name tags and place cards, will provide your guests with sure anxiety relief. (It's comfortable to know "who's who and when what happens where.") [Ed: There she goes again...]

Gifts, Favors and Souvenirs: My philosophy is strong in this area. I believe that money is better spent on giving a token gift to each guest than say, for an expensive band or outrageously expensive decorations—both elements that fade away into the night. Gifts needn't (in most cases, can't) be expensive. As you can see in this budget there was $3.00 allocated. Ideas for gifts or favors in this price range are: Special Polaroid photo in moderately priced frame, ceramic mug customized with message, photo or logo, personalized address or date book, candy in reusable tin, personalized note pads (each person's first name is printed on a small pad) and pen. There are many, many more and if they are beautifully wrapped and either placed at their dinner seat or given as they leave it is a final and permanent way to say, "Thank you for being with us." Scope out a wholesale outlet for these gifts so that you can get $6.00 gifts for $3.00. (See RESOURCES, Chapter 29) To find some good ideas for souvenir items such as photos, buttons, shirts, etc. (See ENTERTAINMENT/ MUSIC, Chapter ll).

Budget Principles

The following principles for allocating your event budget are effective for almost every type of event.

✳ Be practical and conservative about what is "consumed" (food and beverage).

✳ Be generous and caring about what is "given" (favors, gifts and souvenirs)

✳ Be personal and professional with what "invites, organizes or documents" (name tags, place cards , programs and photos).

✳ Be creative and ecological about what "decorates" (floral decor, props, decorations, serving ware).

✳ Be selective and assertive about what "entertains" (music and talent) and who "helps" (servers and services).

✳ Careful and thorough about the "site."

✳ Setting a budget and staying within it are both challenging; by careful and creative planning both are very possible.

Notes & Numbers

~Chapter~

10

Invitations

THE OFFERS THEY CAN'T REFUSE

"Y'all come" written on a corn cob, or "The honour of your presence" engraved on crisp vellum are just two widely diverse ways to ask people to come out for an event. It's all a matter of individual style and there are no longer any rules. The big thing to remember is that the better the invitation the better the turnout. If your invitation smacks of fun, and is loaded with promise, your guests are more likely to make a special effort to attend. At least, they will put your party date on their calendar. (Or, more likely, use a cutesy magnet to attach your invitation to the refrigerator door.)

Invitations do more than inform the guests of the time and place. From casual to classic, the style of the invitation communicates the tone of your party which is a big help to your guests. Using the elegant art of calligraphy to address your invitations adds a definite note of formality and specialness.

In designing your invitation let your imagination soar. If you're not the creative type get help from someone who is and you will wind up with a great invitation.

Match the invitation to your event theme or mood by this rule of thumb:

If it is a very casual affair, given with almost no notice you can simply make a phone call. If you have lots of calls to make, have a friend or two help out.

On the other end of the scale, if it is a formal event you must send a formal invitation that includes a request to respond by mail or phone. (If it is four weeks or closer to a formal event date, it is advisable to send a "reserve-this-date" postcard ahead of your invitation.) Two weeks before your event, it is mandatory to call guests that have not responded, in order get a count for a food guarantee to your caterers.

Stock Invitations

The selection of ready-made invitations is endless. Your town will have dozens of invitation vendors listed in your Yellow Pages, but the best way to select your invitation resource is to ask a friend or family member for a referral. Your invitation resource will be very important to you. You will look to this professional for a wide variety of invitation books from which to select, expert advice on the proper wording, general invitation etiquette and a guarantee of on-time shipment. If you were especially impressed with a certain invitation that you received, get the name of the book from which it was ordered. By using another's invitation purchasing experience you are assured of fair prices, good service and a reputable business. (See RESOURCES, Chapter 29)

Tip: Most invitation suppliers give a 20% discount on printed party goods.

Original Invitations

Unique items that can be used as invitations: Printing on, or attaching your invitation to, unusual items assures that they will stand out from the "ho-humdrum" typical ones that are so often received. The item can be useable, edible, wearable or laughable.

Your message printed on: T-shirts, hats, visors, socks, kerchiefs, frisbees, beach balls, kites, letter openers, refrigerator magnets, Post-It Notes, calendars, mugs, glasses, pennants, pens and pencils, note pads, popcorn bags, shopping bags, plastic bags, ribbons, shoestrings, shoe bags, barf bags (oops! just seeing if you're paying attention) [Ed: I was!] and an endless list of items that have a suitable space available for imprinting your message.

Your message attached to: (hanging from or affixed to) Bags of popcorn, candy, gum, comic books, newspapers, travel brochures, framed photos, small toys, sunglasses, cookies, date books, flashlights, key chains and dozens more.

Items attached to your paper invitation: Feathers, Band-aids, paper clips, stickers, candy or gum, imprinted ribbons (one of my pets), toothpicks, Q-Tips, photos, popcorn kernels, hairnet, bobby pins, samples of tanning lotions or other cosmetics, yarn, tinsel, sequins, labels (wine, food, household products), fabrics, flowers, straw, seed packs, string, lace, cartoons, mini-packs of: aspirin, Sweet-n-Low's, salt & pepper, sugar and myriad other packets that are tiny and mailable (thank goodness for the padded envelope).

Where to find: padded envelopes, most paper and party stores now carry these in several different sizes.

Printed on unusual papers: Accounting, blueprint, want ads, foil or checkproof, telephone, wallpaper, legal pads (or any paper connected to an occupation), maps, tissue, (even T.P. if it's a very casual affair and you want to start with a laugh) brown paper bag, computer, newsprint, cardboard, wrapping paper, transparency, butcher or grocery paper, notebook paper, mylar and fancy writing paper.

Invitations sent in unique containers: Pizza boxes, cassette cases, tubes, padded envelopes, various sized corrugated boxes, record album covers, odd sized envelopes, wildly colored envelopes, cloth bags, [Ed: Here comes that barf bag again.] Zip-Lock bags, film cans, special tins, and here is one of my all-time favorites—in a fortune cookie (See RESOURCES, Chapter 29,)Plastic bottles (ketchup, mustard, baby), plastic envelopes and plastic tubes are becoming popular for sending dimensional invitations. You can see through them to what's inside, and it can be mailed (as is) with a label and stamps.

Where to find: Pizza Boxes, in Yellow Pages under *Pizza Supplies*

Theme Ideas for Invitations

NOEL OLE!

For a Holiday Mexican Fiesta party we printed the invitation on yellow paper, cut in the shape of an Inca sun and glued it to a real tortilla shell. which , in turn, was glued to a tissue-covered cardboard pizza round. We used brightly colored tissue, vivid flower stickers and festive colored ribbons as trimmings. (My trusty pizza box made a perfect mailer for this unique invitation.) The mailing label was plain white, gayly decorated with flower stickers and addressed with colored markers; it was about as inviting as you can get. Needless to say, the Senors and Senoritas said *"Si Si."*

AIN'T THIS SWEET?

An extravaganza of an invitation was an old fashioned, beautifully lettered Valentine, mounted

64

on a white paper doily, trimmed with delicate lace and red satin ribbons. Attached to the inside of the ubiquitous pizza box lid was a red satin bow tie and a string of twirlin' pearls that were labeled "costume starters" for this Roaring Twenties costume party. It turned out that this "offer" could not be refused by any real flapper or dapper.

MOST ELIGIBLE

A singles' bash called for a unique and attention-getting invitation, so we printed the message on the first page of a "little black book" and mailed it in a padded envelope. The guests were provided with pencils and attempted to fill their books with hot numbers. The name of the host nightclub was written in its appropriate place for ready reference.

CLASSIFIED INFORMATION

An invitation to one of the currently popular mystery-type parties was sent in an elegant black envelope regally addressed in gold ink. It contained a neatly typed note directing the guests to read the personal ads in the daily paper for their next mysterious message. The ad revealed a phone number for the guests to call to hear the third clue. Upon calling, a very mystifying customized recorded message contained the pertinent information and the secret password greeted them and instructed them to leave their RSVP.

Note: The voice mail RSVP idea is a time saver when you don't want all of the calls to come into our office or home...especially if you are planning a surprise. It gives you a chance to get "cute" with the message to further perpetuate your theme and you can call in to pick up the messages at your convenience. It is available through your local telephone answering service.

A live answering service is suggested if you are using the R.S.V.P. call to establish menu choices or need to give specific instructions. The cost is not much more than the voicemail.

CATCH THE MAGIC BEFORE IT DISAPPEARS!

The art work on this invitation pictured a tuxedoed torso, one arm extended with a piece of silky tissue tucked into the sleeve. When the tissue was pulled it opened, to reveal the word "pouf" which was written in glitter so that just a bit of magical dust sprinkled out. The color of this tissue determined the prize that the guest would win when presenting it at the event. This award-winning invitation was a self-mailer that, when folded in the right way would stand up. It is rumored that as a tribute to the design of this invitation some of the guests have it displayed on their desk. This was a good example of how some extra finely detailed handwork created the result of "going all out" to make an offer.

Note: That magic invitation started my reputation of designing invitations in the philosophy of the AA program—they always have 12 Steps! (Some of my best and loyal friends have since requested that I NOT invite them to help with any of my "inviting"!)

Fun with Invitations

✻ The invited guests were requested to send back a sample of their handwriting. Those samples were analyzed by an expert and the results provided an ice-breaking activity. A brief analysis/description was written on each name tag in place of a name. Guests tried to match descriptions to guests names that were posted on a master list. As a favor and entertaining activity a more detailed analysis was offered by the handwriting expert at the event.

✻ An actual theme related jigsaw puzzle piece was included in each invitation. Upon arrival, each guest was directed to a table where a completed puzzle was laid out with several pieces missing. The winners were the holders of the pieces that fit into the blanks. This will work with any size party. If you have more pieces than guests, just pull the extras to make sure they are not prize pieces. Purchase two identical puzzles and put the duplicate together.

Note: You can create a custom puzzle by taking a special photo to your photo processing store for them to cut into the desired amount of puzzle pieces.

❋ In this situation each invitation included a cartoon without a caption. The guests were instructed to make up a caption and bring the completed cartoon to to be posted, along with some real cartoons that had been dummied up to look like guest entries. The object of the contest was to guess which cartoons were the real ones and to vote for the best. Grand prizes went to the persons who guessed the real cartoons as well as the persons who's original captions got the most votes. This was an opportunity for the guests to show some real ingenuity.

Split Personality Invitations

❋ In this case the wedding invitation was a very formal and elegant, white on white. However, the reception was to be a luau (splashy, festively floral and informal), so a delicate silk flower with tiny leaves was attached to the reception card. It was just the right touch to establish the mood.

It is true: the smallest gesture can make a terrific impact if it is well thought out and carefully executed. If you are planning to do something like this with your invitation, ask the opinion of three people: One that knows you very well, one that does not know you well, and one that does not know you at all. Their observations will be diverse and from them you should be able to decide exactly what is right to do. While you do want to be clever or unique, you do not (I think) want to be bizarre.

Note: If the invitation to a business event serves as an announcement as well, it is desired that it will be saved and better, yet, passed around. Through its uniqueness you may accomplish this goal. In the publishing business it is called "pass-on" readership. Make good use of white space when you are designing this type of invitation/promotional piece. Creatively and subtly include your commercial, so to speak.

Food for Thought: Remember the last time you received an invitation or announcement that had a different twist, an attachment or a clever presentation? You held it, showed it, saved it, and may still have it. What was there about it that made you feel that you couldn't part with it, let alone ignore it? That's the secret to success in the invitation business. (Forgive me if I get carried away with this invitation stuff, but, getting carried away is not only my job, it's my way of life.)

Now for some A(verage) to Z(any) ideas for invitation gimmicks:

Attachment items and some related catch phrases. (Keep in mind that groaning is good for you.)

Aspirin pack:	"He'll take two before retiring"
	"Plan ahead...for a great party"
	More A's: Alka Seltzer
Balloon:	"We'll take your breath away"
	"Celebrate the high cost of inflation"
	More B's: Band-Aid, bubble gum, buttons and bows
Coin:	"To coin a phrase"
	(or) "It makes cents...."
	More C's: candle (birthday), coupon, charms, caps (as in cap gun)
Diamond	(a rhinestone, unless you're very wealthy):
	"A gem of a party..."
	"If you carat all...."
	More D's: Doily, doodles, diary page, dental floss
Eraser:	"There's no mistake..."
	"Correct me if I'm wrong...."

More E's: Excelsior (packing stuff) "Something of value...."

Essence: perfume samples

Fringe: "It is one of the benefits of working here...."

Feather: "Birds of a feather...."

More F's: fur, foil, film, fishing lure

Gold: (ribbon, foil or chain)

"Worth her weight in...."

"Your golden opportunity...."

More G's: gum, gauze, glitter

Horoscope: "A party in your future..."

"A star was born..."

More H's: hook 'n eye, honey packets, highlighting pens

I.O.U.: "Your Marker for a Super Party"

More I's: index card, I.D. card, initials of stickers, paper or felt

Jigsaw Puzzle: "You'll make the picture complete..."

71

More J's: jelly bean, jingle bell, jewels

Key: "Lock in this date..."

More K's: kiss (candy), knife (plastic)

Lam'e: "No Lam'e excuses accepted..."

More L's: lace, lure, Life Saver, lead (as in, "Get the ...... out...")

Message Slip: Fill in the "While You Were Out" blank with the invitation.

More M's: mirror, mint, macaroni, magnet

Noodle: "Use yours and come to...."

More N's: nail, name tag, nickel

Ornament: "Come hang one on...." (for holiday party; use flat or folding ornament)

Pretzel: "Here's a new twist..."

More P's: pasta, Post-It Note, pull tab

Q-Tip: "Stick it in your ear...."

"Here's a cute tip...."

Rubber band:	"It was a stretch, but we made it...."
	More R's: rice, reinforcements, ribbons, Rolodex cards
Shoestring:	"Tie the knot..."
	"String along with us...."
	Other S's: straw, swizzle stick, sequins, slides, stickers of all kinds
Tea bag:	"Take a dip with us..."
	"Something is brewing...."
	More T's: golf tee, toothpick, token, ticket (any kind), tape
Upholstery :	"$5.00 will cover your seat...."
	More U's: UPC Code bar: "You're priceless..."
Vine (ivy leaf):	"It's on the grapevine...."
	"Watch us grow...."
	More V's: vitamin pill, Velcro, veiling

Wire:	"You're a real live wire...."
	More W's: wishbone, whistle or watch (toy)
X-Rays	??(I'm reaching here)
Yo Yo:	"After all the ups and downs...."
	More Y's: yeast packet, yarn
Zipper:	"Zip your lip...it's a surprise..."
	Last Z: zirconia (Hey! This wasn't E-Z!) [Ed : ZZZZZZzzzzzzz]

All sorts of other items from A to Z are available in catalogs (see RESOURCES: Chapter 29,) The most popular of these items are tiny toys, such as watches, whistles, sunglasses and hundreds of other items, mostly made of plastic. They cost about three cents apiece.

Special paper idea:

If you are celebrating a retirement, promotion, new job or anything employment-related an interesting invitation can be printed on checkproof paper. Make the check payable to the invited guest for services rendered as a "perfect guest", "great employee" or "super customer". Mail this specially printed check "offer" in a window envelope with a priority sticker on the front.

Another retirement-type invite is one printed on an official time card or an employee review form.

Hint: Upon the receipt of an R.S.V.P. from an out of town guest, send them an enthusiastic information letter matched to your invitation or theme. A neatly typed or printed notice giving a complete itinerary of events, predicted weather forecast, hotel and transportation information. Invite your guests to let you know if they have any special requests to make their stay more comfortable.

Recycling hint:

When I receive an invitation envelope, with my name beautifully lettered on it I just can't throw it away. Instead, I take it to my quick print shop and have the calligraphy reproduced on colored notepaper that is sold with matching envelopes.

Printing the envelope with a return address is optional. For just a few dollars I have a set of lovely personal stationary.

Another must:

After you have created one of these wonderful invitations with an attachment or special gimmick design make a mock-up (you needn't use the actual paper or exact items—they need only be similar weight, size or durability,) pack it up as you plan to, and mail it to yourself. Do this step before you order and purchase any of the components of your proposed design. After the package or envelope goes through the mail, you may find that certain things may have to change to make it feasible.

Stamp suggestions:

✳ Double sided tape works well for affixing stamps so that they do not separate from unusual papers.

✳ Always use the prettiest or most attractive stamp on your invitations. Try to color or theme coordinate.

✳ Never run personal invitations through the postage meter.

✳ Bulk rate stamps look better than postage meter. It will take a little longer to affix them, but your invitation will look more personal.

Label, Label...Lose the Label!

Sorry, guys, but hand addressing is always advisable and preferable. Never use a label on an invitation to a personal party, open house or customer appreciation. The "death of the party" is the automatically "slapped-on" label. It is always possible to find people to address envelopes at a minimum wage. Find someone with good handwriting to recruit some friends and supervise the job. My favorite "gray graphic-group" is one of apt and active seniors. (I could never be as "cute" as I am with my "twelve step" invitations if it weren't for their patience and preciseness in implementing my invitation designs.)[Ed: By the time we finish this book, I may be ready for that group...it's safer work.]

For formal invitations, calligraphy is wonderful. (See PARTY POOLING, Chapter 19). You can get calligraphy addressed envelopes by computer for a bit less than by hand. It is "letter perfect" and very hard to detect from the hand done. Expect to pay from 70 cents to $1.00 for each envelope addressed by hand or computer.

✳ To complement your hand-designed invitation you can have your return address printed on (100 is the price break) matching envelopes for little more than the cost of plain envelopes. If you need less than 100, order matching blank paper to make up the difference and you will have some stationery with personalized envelopes. Most print shops have a nice selection of papers with matching envelopes.

✳ Some print shops run colored ink on certain days of the week. You can achieve inexpensive two-color (or more) printing by having your piece run on the appropriate color days. This is very prudent for posters, programs and invitations for charitable causes.

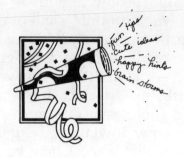

Suggested Mailing Times:

Very formal invitations:

6 weeks lead. See a proof or set a delivery date for 2 weeks before that to allow for error correction time or (in rare instances with a professional) reprinting. These printing mistakes could put you way behind schedule if you do not allow for them.

Birthday or anniversary, graduation:

4 weeks lead. It may be necessary to send a "Save this date" postcard to out-of-town guests a few weeks earlier.

Theme or fund raising event:

Five to six weeks lead. A follow-up phone call three weeks out will increase turnout.

Business event:

10-14 days lead. A phone call reminder and request for an RSVP.

Seminar/convention:

12 weeks lead with two or three tickler postcards

Casual event:

2 weeks. Invitation by mail or phone call should be followed up with phone call for RSVP

Formal—Last Minute:

Phone call to extend invitation, followed up with printed invitation. Also make a phone call to get RSVP if necessary.

Regrets Only pitfalls: It is safer to ask that all guests R.S.V.P. one way or another. You will then be able to call those guests that have not responded and make sure that they did all receive an invitation. "Regrets only" will provide no way of knowing if any guests DID NOT receive their invitations.

Invitation Resources

✳ I am listing the names of some nationally known designers of fabulous customized invitations. Most of these invitations will cost considerably more but they are works of art that will get a tremendous response from your guest list. Send for samples and prices before you rule this out. (see RESOURCES, Chapter 29).

✳ To track down someone in your town that has invitation design talents, contact your School of Art and Design, invitation supplier or popular event planner.

Maps and Directions: Request a professionally drawn map from your event site to print either on your invitation or on a separate sheet of closely matched paper. Important: (Especially if your invitation is very formal.) Do not use a home drawn map. Most desktop publishers can design one for you on their computers. You can share this map with fellow residents if it is a map of your apartment or office complex.

Hand Delivering Invitations

If you go to the trouble of hand-delivering an invitation, go one step further and have the deliverer dressed to fit your theme or image. For a few extra dollars you can hire an extroverted non-actor or a "between engagements" real actor to don a special get-up. A driver/deliverer team is most efficient if they have to go into a downtown area where parking is a hassle.

News item: Statistics show that the most frequently read piece of mail is the standard postcard. If you are on a tight budget, never fear, your well designed and professionally printed invitation or announcement will be not only efficient but effective on a hand-addressed postcard.

FINALE: THE PERFECT INVITATION

The object is to appeal to the seven senses: sight, smell, taste, touch, sound (and my two add-on's, humor and order.) This fabulous Fifties invitation hit each sense.

SIGHT:

It was a standard greeting card fold, featuring a four-color photo of a classic jukebox customized with the company name.

TOUCH, SMELL, TASTE:

Attachment was a stick of Juicy Fruit Gum on the inside left cover.

HUMOR:

Catch phrase: "We want `chew' to come!" printed under the stick of gum.

ORDER:

Clearly printed invitation and announcement (listing products and services) on inside right cover.

SOUND:

Computer chip played "Rock Around the Clock" when card was opened.

This ultra-sensory invitation was truly an event planner's dream come true.

It's time to stop writing about my favorite subject--
invitations. I thought I could not say too much
about the subject. I hope that you agree, since I
said so much. Follow some of these instructions,
tips, hints, and ideas and I guarantee that you will
have a great invitation and a wonderful turnout.

Caution: Be forewarned, one hazard of sending a
perfectly smashing invitation is....the pressure is
on to have a perfectly smashing party! Don't forget
to invite me. [Ed: Me too!]

Notes & Numbers

Notes & Numbers

~*Chapter*~

11

Entertainment

THE LIFE OF THE PARTY

When you have all of the basics for your event together and it looks like you're ready for a perfect party, make sure you've hired some of the people that I always term "the life of the party." These are people with special talents or providers of unique services who will add a certain spark to an already "nice" affair by breaking the ice, providing entertainment, and creating gifts and favors. In other words—people who keep things lively and moving.

Caricaturists: Not only do they provide fascinating entertainment for all of the guests, but their clever sketches make super favors. You can customize these drawings in advance by printing a personal message on the artist's sketch paper and incorporating the sketch made at the event for a very charming gift.

One neat idea is to have a caricature of the guest of honor printed on half of each sketch sheet with a cartoon bubble saying, "Glad you could help me celebrate my 40th, _____." (or suitable saying) During the party, the guest's caricature is drawn and his/her name filled in to complete a superb memento.

Face Painters: There was a time when I associated face painters with kids' parties. They are still a tremendous favorite with children, but the "big" kids love them, too. The most austere, formal occasion will come to life when everyone bears a lively and colorful mini-drawing on a cheek, shoulder, arm or chin. Big and little ladies love paintings of delicate flowers, butterflies, birds and color-coordinated designs that match their party outfits. It is like a painted-on piece of jewelry. Men, on the other "arm" go for the tattoo effect with cartoon characters, scars, and clever sayings. The face painting process is fun to watch and the result increases the "face value" *(oops, it just slipped out)* of the event.

Computer Printouts: "What happened the day you were born?" is the question, and your guests can get the answer on a crisp (suitable for framing) sheet. The computer is housed in Robots, Old Tyme paper stands, or any of other attention-getting facades. The certificate can also be personalized with a headline such as: "Star Discovered at Matt's Bar Mitzvah!"

Where to Find: You may have to call a local computer store or one of the big hotels in your area to seek help from the sales and catering staff. They usually hear about these unique services. Convention center staff may also assist you in your search. Party planners will be helpful, too.

For mail order information on these printouts (See RESOURCES, Chapter 29).

Photo Buttons: Everyone loves to have their picture "took," especially if they are in costume or formal wear. One of the cutest gimmicks that, once again, provides a form of entertainment and produces an amusing party favor is the making of computerized or Polaroid photo buttons. Ask the photographer (or is it computographer?) to bring along the tiny magnets that attach to the back of the button and then...abracadabra! the button can be worn and then later used as a refrigerator decoration. (I love these little winners.)

Where to Find:Call a face painter, caricaturist or local art store. Check under Buttons in the Yellow Pages.

Special Photos, Backdrops or Custom Frames: Another way to keep the natives from becoming too restless is to photograph them behind those funny fotoboards. This could be an existing board, or you may have one customized to suit your theme. Another way to go is to hire a Victorian photographer or a Celebrity Photo company. These gimmick photos are very realistic, lots of fun to take and good for impressing your pals. You can purchase picture frames in hundreds of styles from light cardboard to lucite. Almost any frame material can be engraved, etched or imprinted for a totally custom favor.

Where to Find: Specialty photographers call a local photographer. Shopping mall promotional directors usually have these names on file.

Fortune Tellers/Readers: Your guests will stand in line to get a chance to peer into their future with the guidance of either a card, tea leaf, palm, tarot card or handwriting reader/analyst. These mystical happenings can be taking place throughout the event and not interfere with other activities. (They can raise "fortunate" funds for you, too, if you charge a nominal fee for them.) It is one of those whimsical treats that can be taken as seriously as desired.

Where to Find: Your local New Age shop will have a long list of readers psychic and analysts as well as experts who will speak to your group.

Costumed Characters: No self-respecting black tie affair takes place without at least one Teenage Mutant Ninja Turtle pouring punch, a gorilla taking coats or a Dolly Parton serving snacks. Outfitting the staff in authentic butler and French maid costumes adds a touch of classy mirth. The more incongruous the get-up, the more spontaneous the fun. The occasional put-on party crasher; the "plant"that is an incessant bore, nerd or computer geek, the hired "klutzy" server and the feuding family are all shocking, surprising and definitely stimulating. The party is never the same after these fabulous characters make their appearances. Whether they deliver a special message or simply add color, these unforgettable guests make an impression...good or bad.

Where to Find: Most will be discovered in the Yellow Pages under "Entertainers," either as an individual talent or with an agency. Another way to find them is to call the local party store for suggestions or stop in and check out their bulletin board. Also try singing telegram services, local comedy clubs, etc.

Barbershop Quartets: An energetic break for any event is the impromptu performance of a "super singer times four." These foursomes, male or female, are all very professional, entertaining and talented. Their amateur standing permits them to charge only a limited fee, like a donation to a fund for their group.

Where to Find: Call your local Chamber of Commerce for the name and number of a good quartet.

Crash Ballroom Dance Course: Local ballroom dance schools will send an instructor couple out to your event to give mini lessons in the latest dance craze. The great thing about this is that the guests who want to jump in and jive will provide lively entertainment for those that prefer to be wallflowers. If your theme is Island, Hawaiian or tropical, check with the local dance schools. Some will send out several of their more advanced students in grass skirts to run a short course on the "hula-baloo." There will be a small cost, but for a truly authentic luau, it will be well worth it.

Gambling Tables: (You can't lose on this one.) A couple of blackjack tables, roulette wheels and some slots will create a small casino atmosphere without taking over the scene. Another "winner" is the money machine, a booth with swirling and whirling bills (real or bogus) just waiting for someone to step in and grab them. (The bogus bills can be used to buy prizes or activities at a fund raiser or party.) These gaming items can be rented by the hour, evening with or without operators.

Where to Find: In the Yellow Pages under "Games & Game Supplies."

Unusual Solo Musical Instruments: In our town we are lucky to have our own Organ Grinder. You might, too. Charming and picturesque music puts guests into a festive, nostalgic and happy mood. Unique instrumentals are subtle and fit in anywhere, but are an especially delightful surprise at a formal affair. Other instruments that are unexpected and enjoyable are: autoharp, harmonica, concertina, mandolin, xylophone, ukelele, clavichord. Any of these rarely-heard-as-solo instruments will create not only background music but interesting conversation, too. Go for the gusto with a soloist on tuba or oboe.

Where to Find: Local Musicians Union, music school or music store referrals.

Silhouettes: This will take you back to grade school and those little black paper cutouts in their cardboard frames that you brought home to grace Mom & Dad's dresser. Well, artists who create them still do exist, so for a novel twist have it done at your party and you and your guests can give it to your kids for their dressers. It may seem like a lost art, when your search shows that these artists are difficult to find, but the search will be worth it. (Perhaps you should hang out at the black construction paper department...just kidding.)

Where to Find: Arts and crafts supply store. Ask the clerk for ideas. You may find the name of these artists with the management of local art festivals, too.

Personalities and Celebrities: The inclusion of scintillating, interesting and wonderful people on your guest list, such as media celebrity-types, authors, experts in most any field, inventors and entrepreneurs, people with unusual occupations and professional party animals (those that love the opportunity to get together with people...for any reason) will always add life to your party.

Where to Find: Celebrity agencies, local writers' groups, radio and television stations, networking with friends.

The outrageously popular Karaoke (Sing Along) Machine can make a good singer sound unbelievable and the mediocre singer sound pretty good. Unfortunately, the lousy singer will still sound lousy, but will be wholesome comedic entertainment for all. Professionally recorded backup music, blended with the singer's raw talent, amplified through state-of-the-art equipment sounds almost broadcast quality. The entire performance is viewed on a monitor or a big screen for a larger, more dramatic effect. Any type of gathering literally, comes alive with this phenomenon. Kids and adults of all ages find just the right song to sing from the thousands of tunes available. As a lasting gift or favor, your guests can take home a music video of their performance that will provide them with hours of viewing enjoyment. Great business promotion or fund raising activity.

Where to Find: To obtain the number of your local Karaoke agent you can call (612)544-7441.

Magicians, mimes, and jugglers: The performances of these casual acts, sometimes called "street performers" will liven up your event. Without commanding attention from your group as a whole, these professionals will move amongst your guests giving private shows to a small group of guests. Or they can be located on a small platform to put on mini-shows for the milling and moving guests. Colorful, dynamic, friendly and entertaining talent of this kind fits for occasions both formal and casual.

Where to Find: Performers, such as jugglers, mimes, sword swallowers and other street and carnival talent can be found through talent agencies, theater groups, and renaissance festival management.

Notes & Numbers

Notes & Numbers

~Chapter~

12

Guest Comfort

ARE WE HAVING FUN YET?

The most important ingredient of a winning entertaining experience is concern for the comfort of your guests. Starting with designing the invitation, your essential goal is to increase well-being among your guests. At every point, focus on reduction of the potential for anxiety by increasing guest awareness of when, where, what and how—whenever possible.

We've called it "hospitality," but it's a certain mutual good feeling that is shared by host and guest. No matter how elaborate the party, how elegant the decor or how glorious the food, if your guests aren't comfortable, it is not going to be a successful event.

Have you ever been to a function where the most vivid recollection of the event is of the unbearable wait in the buffet line, the crowd at the bar or the slow and inadequate meal service? You may as well save the money that you plan to spend for the ice sculpture, the chocolates with your name on them or the band's authentic big band sound!! The guests will forget all about those luxury items if they experience great discomfort.

This chapter should give you most of the *Helpful Hospitality Hints* that you'll need to enhance guest comfort throughout your celebration.

Start with an invitation which lets your guests know:

- What the dress code will be.
- What food will be served, (dinner, hors d'oeuvres, dessert, brunch, breakfast, lunch.)
- What guests can bring (food, beverage, another guest)
- What the gift policy is. (Even if you say "No gifts," some will still bring them). In order to establish "no *real* gifts" use the phrases "goofy gifts," "gag gifts," or one that I liked was "a gift to make him laugh or cry." That left it wide open.

  Note: A very meaningful gift policy for a personal special occasion is to making it a charitable gesture by requesting that each guest bring a toy or book for a child or senior. This is a way you can spread the joy of a special occasion to many others, well beyond the date.

✳ How to get there. Include a clear map. Be sure to put your phone number and the number of the event site on the map.

✳ The times scheduled for special activities or presentations. If you are planning some special entertainment or a tribute, state the exact time that it will occur so that your guests can make a serious attempt to be present for the main festivities.

✳ Make it known that they are welcome to stop by for just a portion of the event. It allows them to graciously accept your invitation even though they have a prior commitment. This will be especially true of weekend nights when most major events take place and the competition for their time is keen. (Popularity can be mighty frustrating, can't it?) Including the schedule of activities helps your guests to select a section of the event that they can attend.

✳ In addition to a map, provide signage and directional help: Place clear signs, balloons, banners or some other identifying item on street posts, trees or fences (at easy to see eye level.) Mark the appropriate turns so that your guests will always know that they are on track.

✳ Typically, it's easier for the driver to follow road signs than to read a map while driving. If it's nighttime, use arrows of reflecting tape as directional markers. Of course, your porch lights must be on, and a few luminaries (candles in paper bags weighted with sand) will help on the walkway. (RESOURCES, Chapter 29).

- Use extra lighting for dark passages or stairways. Apartment dwellers: Don't limit your signage to the front door of your building. Use a series of signs to lead your guests through the hallway, into the elevator and right up to your unit door or to the party room, as the case may be.

- Creative and funny "party starting" sayings or a-word-at-a-time punch lines (a la Wall Drug) make effective signs. This use of signage is also suggested for events in a hotel or banquet facility. Post attractive (not makeshift or poorly printed) signage in the garage, elevator, hallways and at main entrances to help decrease guest anxiety. Well placed people can also make great directional markers as "living signs" that convey a message such as a code word, a line of a song, or a catch phrase that supports your theme.

- *Bonus Idea:* (This really belongs in the name tags chapter, but you might miss it there.) If you live in an area that is extremely difficult to find, make name tags in the form of a humorous "medal of honor" award that is presented for success in finding the place.

✳ The ultimate welcoming signal is the searchlight or klieg light used at Hollywood Premier nights. Your guests will find you very easily and they'll feel like glamorous celebrities as they make their way up your driveway.

Where to Find: "Searchlights" in your Yellow Pages

Greeters and Meeters: One of the most awkward moments is arriving at the gala party destination and, alas, there's no one to greet you. You stand with your coat in your hand, not knowing for sure if you're in the right place or what to do next. In addition to festive and attractive signage to get guests to the door, cordial and knowledgeable greeters are a real boon to fine hospitality.

Instant guest comfort can be created by having someone say, "Hello, welcome to the Brown party! May I take your coat?" or "You will find the check room over there, Mr. Jones, then come back so I can give you your name tag". these goodwill ambassadors can, after greeting them and registering them, direct them to the next stop, which may be the bar, the reception line or dining tables. This concept is especially helpful for weddings, parties, business occasions, open houses and reunions. When you make your plan, arranging for cordial and qualified "greeters" is essential to keep things gracefully moving along at your function.

Name tags and Place cards: There is a whole chapter on this subject, but from a guest comfort standpoint, the basics are:

❋ Name tags create a level of comfort for guests at every type of function. (This includes weddings, anniversaries, parties and open houses.)

❋ Print the names in large bold block print (ahead of time if possible)

❋ Do not let guests do their own tags or they will be difficult to read.

❋ At business events add a company name; and include the relationship to the honoree on the name tags for private functions. (Eg.,, "Patty's sister," "Patty's Mom.)

❋ Place cards take the anxiety out of finding a place to sit at buffet or sit down dinners.

❋ Cards should be clearly printed and placed on the reception table in alphabetical order to allow guests to fine their card easily.

❋ Using place cards allows you to mix and match your guests to encourage new acquaintances and avoid cliques.

❋ Reserve accessible seating for your elderly, ill or handicapped guests. Use a huge bow, a special banner or sign to mark these seats. It will save awkwardness of having to relocate others to accommodate arriving guests with special needs.

Tip: An all-time favorite buffet line "comfort/convenience" item is the serving plate that has an indentation to hold a stem glass or stemmed cup. One can stand in a crowded room, hold food and beverage and eat gracefully and comfortably without doing an Ed Sullivan show balancing act. These plates or trays are available in snack or dinner size and are very attractive (and mostly inexpensive). Most are disposable plastic, but they also come in durable acrylic for a sturdy reusable family staple item that can be shared. (See PARTY POOLING , Chapter 19) (See RESOURCES: Chapter 29,

Another buffet line "do" is giving each table a number and calling tables in turn by numbers to alleviate standing in long waiting lines. (see BUFFETS, Chapter 22)

Valet Parking: If you can afford it (See PARTY POOLING, Chapter 19) one of the most generous, thoughtful and hospitable things you can do for your guests is to have their cars parked for them. As a Minnesota party animal who has seen parties ruined by the weather and its ravages upon gowns,

hairdos, tuxedos, costumes, and temperaments...
(and that was just making the short trip from the
parking lot to the front door.) I strongly urge that
you insure that your guests start the affair in a
good mood and in good shape, no matter what the
weather.

Reminiscing now: One of my fondest "guest comfort"
party ideas was hiring a crew of "Valets from the
Ballet" (burly football players wearing fluffy pink
tutus.) for a party that claimed to be "Ticky Tacky,
But Neat," and the "wicky-wacky" festivities all
started with the pirouetting parkers.

Out-of-town guests take extra consideration in your
planning, especially if it's their first visit to your
town. Some of the extras you can provide are mini-
city tours, shopping excursions, beauty make-overs
or baby-sitting.

❋ Your city bus line will have the names of
drivers that serve as tour guides and drivers for
weekend events. You can rent vans or mini-
buses.

❋ Cosmetic line representatives (Mary Kay, for
instance) will give complimentary glamour
make overs at the hotel.

❋ Providing baby-sitters during the wedding
ceremony and reception (or any other event-
related activities) for the younger children
who may get bored; this gives the parents a
chance to enjoy themselves.

When selecting hospitable "in-room" guest gifts keep in mind the following:

❋ For edible gifts choose fruit, nuts, cheese and crackers to tide your guests over from one activity to the next (saves on their room service charges.) Large, bulky gift items such as baskets or buckets are inconvenient if the person in traveling on the plane

❋ One hostess obtained the birthdate of each of her guests. She surprised them with a computer printout of "What happened the day you were born" sheet (rolled up and tied with a ribbon) in their room, on their pillow. It was a thoughtful welcome gift as well as a perfect conversation piece.

❋ The use of two very important words— your guests *first and last names*, imprinted or engraved on a gift will indicate that you are very happy and grateful to have them present. Personalize simple gifts such as matches, note pads and postcards to serve as a gift and welcome guests upon their arrival. A nice bottle of wine with a customized wine label is a beautiful and gracious gift.

Light and sound: must be adjusted to a comfort level. Harsh, bright lights will be uncomfortable for your guests. They will leave at the first possible graceful exit moment ..and probably with a headache. The sound level of the music or entertainment is very "instrumental" (sorry...) [Ed: You're sorry?] in the comfort of your guests. Be aware of the guests shouting at each other, straining to hear each other, you will need to be assertive and request that your band or D.J. turn down the volume. (They are not always thrilled about this request, but it is, after all, your party.)

Remember that the average attention span of party guests is four hours. If you are planning an event such as a wedding, try to regulate the duration from the start of the wedding to the end of the reception, keeping it to not much more than four hours. If your service starts at 7 p.m. your guests will be starting to slow down at 11 p.m. Focus main activities and entertainment for the 8-11 time slot. We have all been to beautiful parties and wedding receptions that lasted too long, the band playing the last set for a handful of people. Remember that your guests started preparing for your event at 4:30 or 5:00 in order to arrive promptly at 7.:00 If they stay until ll:00 they have invested more than 6 hours of their time into your event. In your planning, if you keep the schedule tight and moving right along, you'll be adhering to the wise old show business saying "Leave them wanting more."

Suggestion: If the wedding party has photos or license signing or any details to take care of that will delay them, do not wait for their arrival to start the reception. Open the bar, have some music playing, take video interviews or start serving food. (Or all of the above.) It is a disastrous beginning for an event to have guests waiting uncomfortably, for the party to begin. All dressed up with nothing to do.

Suggestion: If possible, set the location of your reception as close to the wedding ceremony site as possible. One of the major causes of "guest discomfort" is a long drive to the ceremony, that is matched by a longer drive to the reception. If a guest is unfortunate enough to live a great distance from either or both sites, it may be the marathon drive that will be the most memorable part of the day.

Another suggestion: Do anything to avoid scheduling your reception more than 30 minutes after the ceremony ends. In some cases there has been a two or three hour lapse and the inconvenience to the guests has been considerable. When guests are excited and ready to party, do not cause them to wait. Out of towners have nothing to do and the others won't want to do anything else. If you are forced to hold your reception in a less than ideal location, it may, in the long run ,be far better than letting that long delay spoil your party.

A non-smoking rule: It will please 90% of your guests and contribute greatly to their comfort.

One for the road: For daytime outdoor events be sure to locate the receiving line in a shaded place. The bright, hot sun will cause both the wedding party and the guests to wilt.

To lighten up this segment, I pass along the idea of a great hostess and ultimate comfort giver who didn't want her guests to feel awkward about leaving early. (And haven't you felt a little sheepish when leaving the party before it has officially ended?) She posted this sign:

GUESTS' GO-HOME GUIDE

It's this time:	When you hear the host say:
7:30 - 8:30	"Thanks for stopping in."
8:30 - 9:30	"Say "Hi" to the baby sitter (or) enjoy the news!"
9:30 - 10:30	"Sorry you have to work tomorrow"
10:30 - 11:30	"Would you like to come back next Saturday night? "(the perfect party guest)
11:30 - 12:30	"No, really, we don't use that lamp shade much...and it does look great on you..".

| 12:30 - 1:30 | "You really do miss show biz, don't you? 7-11 is still open!" |
| 1:30 - 230 | "Well, we are going to bed and let you poor people go home!" |

As you can see it was o.k. to leave anytime.

I hope I haven't made any of you uncomfortable with these examples of what not to do. It was a lot of discomfort to read about in one sitting. In order to help you do the right thing, though, I had to point out the wrong thing. It's a very uncomfortable job, but someone had to do it!

Notes & Numbers

DRESSED UP WITH SOMEPLACE TO GO

More and more special events call for costumes, formal wear; and themed apparel. "Dress code" is one of the most important bits of information found on a good invitation. Just because the party is on a Saturday night, it doesn't always warrant your wearing "date-night" dress-up clothes. There are several other options that will bring out the flamboyant fashion flair in all guests.

Costume Parties

A theme may dictate that you wear anything from a toga to a tux. As a rule everyone wears exactly what they want to wear...if they can construe it to conform to the guidelines set down by the invitation. Highly creative types will take the designing and assembling of their costumes to extremes, and the results of their efforts will provide top-flight entertainment for other guests. The less inspired will make only a minimal stab at dressing to fit the mode. My "guest comfort" theory allows that each person should be encouraged to get involved at his/her own level, whether it is in vivid day-glo colors (i.e., Lady Godiva or King Arthur) or on the pale end of the spectrum (i.e., a pair of Elvis sunglasses or a Pee Wee Herman bow tie.)

The most common places to find celebration costumes:

✳ Costumes of all designs and intricacy can be rented or purchased from local suppliers.

✳ Dressmakers and designers will start from scratch or alter something.

✳ Scouting around or borrowing from a friend takes little effort and will cost next-to nothing.

✳ Thrift stores and vintage clothing stores are jam-packed with garments just hanging around waiting for a night out on the town.

✳ In some cases the basics of a good costume are in your own closet, attic or basement and need only the magic touch of a "wardrobe wizard" for improvising and devising your "disguising." [Ed: Where was that barf bag, again?]

Here, as in most of the other chapters of this book, I urge you to call upon the most creative and innovative person you know for help. This will be someone who can help you in order to fit the theme, (to utilize an amusing play on words or a gimmick) and then direct you to a right resource to find it. A costume pro can put it all together for the perfect look. Your "pro" could be a student of art or of fashion design, an actor or a makeup/hair stylist (or all three if you really want to win the prize!)

Putting' on the Ritz

With the prevalence of formal banquets, awards ceremonies, fancy balls, and country-club-type events, the formal wear; companies are thriving. Males of all ages who have occasion to get dressed in "monkey suits" at least once a year often find that owning a tuxedo can be very practical. (The going rental rate is about $75.00, so wearing your very "owned" tuxedo just four times would amortize the price (average $300) of its purchase.) Both women and men are wearing tuxes for special occasions [Ed.: Mine has a rhinestone-studded cummerbund and bow tie!]

One for the Dream Category: I flipped over an off-white gaberdine (trimmed with gold braid) tux-with-tails that was displayed in the window of one of the most fashionable women's stores on El Paseo in Palm Desert, California. The price tag read about $3,000. *Now the Scheme:* I'm going to be conservative and creative by buying a new (or very slightly used) set of tails from the rental shop and sew on the gold and glitter myself to make it fabulous, yet frugal.

Glistening gowns, sparkling jewels, and luxurious furs worn with shiny gold or silver pumps are standard uniform for 50% of our social and business/social occasions. Women pounce on any opportunity to get decked out for an appearance in their glamorous garb. 'Tis the fantasy world that beckons to us. These spectacular garments can be purchased new or used, rented or borrowed

Wacky Costume Party Plans

Autograph and Artists Party: Guests dress in white (destined for the Goodwill) garments, either provided by the host or guest. Another possibility for costumes is to send paper dresses or shirts right along with the invitation. Brightly colored pens and markers are either stashed in paint buckets around the party site or strung on a rope necklace around the neck of each guest. Signatures or drawings made by the scribbles, streaks and strokes of these "dabbling" guests will soon cover the once-snowy white costumes. During the festivities, budding artists "works-on-wearables" will be part of a "juried" show and prizes will be awarded to the most promising artist. Painters hats, with guests' names lettered on the front will serve as dandy name tags. By setting up an easel with paints (matching the hosts' interior design color scheme) and brushes for guests to play Picasso or Van Gogh, you commission a work of art as well as a lasting memento of the party.

The menu should be colorful in design: blueberry pancakes, brown rice, green beans, orange juice, red snapper all served to the haunting strains of "Somewhere Over the Rainbow." [Ed: HELP!! No! this is too much!]

Rock Around the Clock: Each guest is instructed to wear clothing that is related to a certain hour of the day. Costumes can represent an activity, song title, phrase, item, occupation, television show or movie that is indicative of the hour or the actual number. Examples: Six a.m. could be represented by a milkman, paper boy, early D.J. or six-pack of beer, six geese a laying, an alarm clock set at Six, etc. The double bonus of this kind of party is that the imagination and ingenuity shown by your guests' costumes provide complete involvement and incredible entertainment. For instance: Use clocks and watches for a theme and activities could be timed races, Time Trivia (song titles, movies, books—with time mentioned in them), music of (here's a plug for my hometown band) The Time. Meals of the hour will make a "timely" menu, i.e., breakfast, brunch, lunch, tea, supper, dinner, midnight snack and the three a.m. "refrigerator raid."

Instant Weekend Get-Away: For this Friday night party invite guests to dress and pack appropriately for their fantasy weekend trip. Hosts, whether individuals, company or organization, arrange for a two day trip (including air fare, hotel and incidentals) that would start the next day. This grand prize is awarded to the couple that dresses and packs most appropriately for the selected destination. In case of duplicates, a final winner is decided by a drawing. The lucky get-away guests can leave early Saturday morning and return Sunday night or opt to take the trip at another time. This is a great fund raising event, if each couple pays a healthy admission fee, the trip is donated so the profits go to charity. Planners must keep the destination a top secret. The authentic foods, music and decor of the possible destinations is not only interesting, but keeps the anxious would-be travelers in suspense.

Gala Wedding Re-enactment To celebrate a special anniversary, invite guest couples to wear their original (or replica) wedding gowns and tuxedos and bring along a photo for comparison. Single guests must borrow a gown or tux from a relative or friend or, as a last resort, rent their costumes. The guests gather first at the home of hosts for the "wedding ceremony" cocktail party and move to another spot for a dinner/dance "reception". During the cocktail hour, guests' automobiles are festooned with "Just Married" signs and tin cans. Photos are taken, "a la Prom time" for a souvenir, videos are taken and shown later. Later at the dinner/dance, typical wedding reception fare is served, balloons and bouquets decorate the "I Do-Re-Do" site as the happy couples dance to music of wedding days gone by.

More Costume Challenges

Tacky Party...(Tasteless and Mannerless)

Horror Movie Characters

Fantasy Occupations

Eras: Roaring Twenties, Forties, Fifties, Sixties and Seventies

Cartoons: Simpsons, Dick Tracy, Peanuts, Superman, Batman

Broadway Show Stars: "Annie", "Sugar Babies", "Cats"

Famous Bad Guys and Good Guys

Potluck and Passports: Bring an ethnic food specialty and dress as the chef

Parade of Years: Costumes represent a renowned event or person of the assigned year

Guest of Honor Look-Alikes: Pick up on hobbies, talents, occupation, physical attributes, etc.(See RESOURCES, Chapter 29)

Frederick's of (name of your street): Outrageous unmentionables and lounge wear

Incredible Edibles: Costumes must be made of edibles (wrapped or unwrapped and worn over basic leotard or swimsuit)

Reincarnation Predictions: What guests want to "come back" as.

Fortunes, Prophecies and Fantasies: Guests dress as gurus, prophets, fortune tellers, etc. (Have some real readers on hand.)

Notes & Numbers

~Chapter~

14

NameTags/PlaceCards

ANXIETY BUSTERS

One of the most embarrassing moments that can happen to a person is being approached by another whose name has temporarily escaped you. No matter whether you are in a business or social situation, the distressful feeling is the same. Not everyone can easily or gracefully admit such a memory lapse. Typically, we grope for words or (admit this, you guys!) avoid talking to "those who remain nameless," and of course, risk being rude.

Then, to add further embarrassment, since you cannot remember this person's name you cannot introduce him/her to your companion. As this mystery person walks away, you say, "I can't believe it...I know his name as well as I know my own." Name tags are not only face-namers...they are face-savers!

More and more brides are requesting name tags to alleviate their own anxiety. The names of aunts, uncles, cousins and neighbors from kindergarten will not stump the smart bride that labels her guests with lovely, specially created name tags. (See RESOURCES, Chapter 29) Reunions are disastrous without proper name tags. Most reunion planners are including a yearbook photo on the name tags for their class.

Now, I'm not talking about the dreary and drab "Hello, my name is..." variety. You can find much more colorful and exciting tags at the variety store, or better yet, recruit your creative resource person to help you design a tag to match your theme or decor. Just add ribbon, lace, stickers, sequins or other trimmings. and your guests won't hesitate to wear them.

Name Tag Nuances:

✳ Send the tags along with invitations for a "think positive" approach.

✳ Print names in large block letters.

✳ Do not *ever* let guests write their own tags.

✳ Personally place a tag on each guest so that she/he will wear it.

Most people do this wrong!

Placement: Near the right shoulder so that it will be in the eye's path when shaking hands.

✳ As a creative replacement for stick-on tags, use unique items such as plastic bibs, award ribbons, headbands or hats, ambassador-style ribbons, decorative medallions hanging from ribbons, or perched on a flower.

✳ Name tags which hang around neck on chains or ribbons prevent delicate fabrics from being damaged by pin or adhesive. They can be made from decorated poster board or any number of other materials.

✳ In addition to name, it is fun to add the guest's relationship to honoree such as "Patty's sister" or "Patty's neighbor." Especially at weddings, where there are two sets of friends, family and associates. For birthday celebrations you can get silly and write things like, "Patty's Grade-school Sweetheart", "Patty's Boss's Boss", (his wife). The name tags then become a source of amusement.

118

✳ Name tags can be used for contests, games. icebreakers and seating instructions.

✳ For an icebreaker effect, in addition to the name, write a secret about the person such as: "collects tinfoil", "won a Yo-Yo championship", wears red socks to bed, or "reads National Enquirer". It doesn't matter if these things are true or not. In fact, part of the contest could be to guess if they are true or false.

✳ Another name tag game is to give each guest a name tag with a famous name written on it. This tag is placed on his/her back. During the course of the party the guest must guess the name on his back by asking "yes or no" questions of the other guests. This idea has been around for years because it is a good one.

✳ Writing the guest's table number on his/her name tag is efficient and alleviates the need for place cards.

WARNING! WARNING!

Do not ever slap a name tag on the fender of a car. A bride that I know cringes when she tells of her guests putting their tags on the "honeymoon car" as they left the reception. What was meant to be a cute prank turned sour since the tags left marks on the car that could *NEVER* be removed.

Now about place cards.

✳ Using them is yet another way to make guests feel more comfortable. Table assignments take the guesswork out of seating. Assigning seating allows you to mix and match guests, thus encouraging fresh conversations and new acquaintances.

✳ Place cards should follow the theme and match the name tags. They can be decorated with a sticker, a tiny piece of ribbon, a small item like a life-saver, button, M&M and so forth.

✳ Place cards should be very clearly and neatly printed, then arranged on the registration table in alphabetical order so that the guests can find theirs easily.

✳ You may also post a decorative seating chart with the guests' names and seat assignments. Here, again, the names should be in alphabetical order.

✳ Make sure that the table numbers are displayed clearly, in large print and preferably elevated for better visibility.

✳ Seat elderly or handicapped guests or those with small children near the exit for their convenience and comfort in leaving and returning.

✳ If you are a computer buff and planning a very large event, there are name tag programs for your PC. Some of them print in several beautiful calligraphy styles and will imprint 1500 tags per minute. Definitely a very efficient and effective tagging system for crowds. They are set up to print place cards, banners and signage, too. (See RESOURCES:, Chapter 29)

Notes & Numbers

~Chapter~

BALLOONS, BOUQUETS & BANNERS

There are thousands of ideas floating around out there for decorating a space for an event. In the old days it was crepe paper and balloons and that was pretty much it. (My dear Mom told me that.) [Ed: Did your Dear Mom ever tell you the story of Pinocchio?] O.K. so I have lived through the eras of cutting up newspaper for confetti to celebrate the end of a war (How's that for honest?) [Ed: Better.] crepe paper, tinsel, shredded cellophane, mylar, confetti guns, balloon drops and now it's smoke pots and laser lights. The extents that you can go to with decorations and effects are awesome and sometimes awfully confusing. I will attempt to give you some decoration direction, although the unrestrained dreamer is the best designer of party decor.

Balloons

These miracles of invention have graced and glorified event sites for hundreds of years. There was a time when balloons were somewhat reserved for kids parties, Halloween and political rallies. It has been some time now since I have been to an event that did not have balloons as the basic decoration item. No other form of decoration can create the atmosphere, fill the space and make the statement that helium or air-filled balloons of latex, plastic or mylar can. With them you can create whimsy, sophistication or downright drama.

It never ceases to amaze me, the marvelous creations that our top balloon designers produce.

Sculptures a mile high, columns, arches, massive drops, airables (giant tubes filled with helium or air that can be draped from the ceilings of huge coliseums to make a giant statement) tiny mylar puffs in dozens of shapes on sticks, unusual shaped mylar balloons that can either shimmer and float above the crowd or stand at attention as a statuesque official greeter of guests.

Huge balloon sculptures can spell out names, form logos, arch over entire rooms, form hallways and tents, stand as columns or statues, and hang from wires in atriums. Incorporating these artistic shapes into the decor of your event will make a dramatic focal point. By using coordinating and matching balloon bunches throughout the room you will fill the room with the color, mood and texture that you desire. You can combine balloons with lights, flowers, streamers, fabric and paper to achieve hundreds of effects that can be used as table decorations as well as on walls, ceilings and windows treatments.

Helium balloons floating loose with shiny mylar ribbons streaming down make a shimmery effect that will last until the end of party. This idea works very well in small rooms (with medium height ceilings) where there isn't room for large balloons displays. It is an easy and inexpensive way to fill a room with instant festivity. You can let the guests take balloons home as souvenirs.

Three or four balloons serve as a centerpiece or table decoration when weighted down with gift wrapped packages, vases, baskets, bottles, bags and any of hundreds of other items that may be functioning as containers or decorative objects. Just this small and simple touch will give the room a gala look.

Shiny or glittery ribbons, lace and trimmings such as tinsel, iridescent shredded cellophane, colored excelsior, sparkling garlands and metallic confetti; tied, wrapped, sprinkled and festooned among balloons will result in sensational and dazzling decorations.

Balloons can be imprinted with the name of your business, your logo, the name of your special event, the guest(s) of honors' name or your personal greeting. Unique and unusual shapes can be ordered or designed to your specifications. These customized balloons are very popular at fund raisers, trade shows, school or college parties to serve as decorations as well as promotional items. These specialty items are available from most balloon suppliers or advertising specialties companies. Imprinting does take several weeks, though, so be sure and order in time. (Rush orders will cost you almost double.)

The latest innovation in the imprinted balloon business is Photoballoons. Your favorite full color photo will be reproduced on 18" or 10" mylar balloons within minutes. It is a good concession to have set up at your major event not only as a give-away but as an entertainment concept.

Weddings, bar mitzvahs, anniversaries and other sentimental occasions are enlightened and "delightened" [Ed: Making up words now?] by shiny jeweltone balloons patterned with flowers, stars, stripes, marbleized, and iridescence. Spraying the insides of clear balloons with confetti and glitter creates a heavenly and enchanting look that will suitably grace tabletops and entry ways to fascinate your guests. In small bouquets or massive sculptures these patterned balloons are elegant and effective.

One of the latest and greatest innovations in "balloonery" is stuffing objects into clear balloons for a variety of visual touches that will pose a mystery for everyone. These unusual displays make long-lasting gifts and decorations since they are filled with air rather than helium. You can present these clever and attractive decorations as prizes at the end of the event and their "stuffings"

125

which could be stuffed animals, (would this make them "twice stuffed"?) [Ed: Keep your mind off mashed potatoes, please.] soft silk flowers, cloth dolls, candy, articles of clothing, and small figurines or art objects will be most well received.

Another dramatic entertainment/decoration concept is filling a huge net, suspended from the ceiling, with air filled balloons to be dropped at a perfect moment to create a large sensation among the guests. Picture this. As hundreds of balloons, of any color or description, float gently down, the enthralling strains of a celebration song fill the room bringing a rousing cheer from the crowd. It is an awesome vision. It takes a special effort to set up a balloon drop but the effect of that moment is spectacular (Keep that video camera rolling to "capture this release.") [Ed: I actually liked that one!]

Those huge hot-air filled balloons that carry folks (around the world in under a hundred days)make fabulous decorations. Tethered (attached, so as not to float) and inflated, they can be a form of entertainment as your guests gather around to take a closer look. Some of them are actual works of art, with their blazing colors and giant designs.

The miniature versions , when carrying a custom banner, are highly (oops!) popular advertising gimmicks and can carry greetings for special events. You can rent them for a day, week or month to shout (it's not really loud) your message from the rooftop for all the world to see. As a decoration or a declaration these inflatable billboards are very effective.

Things to remember when you are hiring a balloon company:

✳ Ask to see their portfolio. Ask the costs of those arrangements that are like what you had in mind.

✳ Ask if they will be using their main staff for your job, or will they be over booked and need to call in the reserves.

✳ Find out if the person that is working with you in the ordering and planning stages will be there the day of your event.

✳ Ask them to make up a sample of the table arrangement and give you a sketch and description of any large sculptures or displays. At that time you can decide if it is exactly what you want.

✳ If they are doing a job soon, ask if you might get permission to peek in on their work either just before or during the event.

✳ Ask if you could save money by helping with some of the assembly. Labor is costly and they

127

might be happy to have the help. Some busy seasons, you will find them working around the clock. If you get involved in your project you may actually lighten their burden on a busy weekend.

✳ If you have seen some impressive designs that you really liked, obtain a photo and bring it to your balloon decorator for estimates on duplication.

Balloon Decorating ideas:

If you are entertaining in your home, use balloons and decorations that coordinate with your decor. The effect will be sensational. anytime, but especially during the holidays, as a fresh approach to festivity.

Mylar balloons make a beautiful welcome statement in the hotel room of guests for your event. They will last for more than the weekend and will spill the celebratory atmosphere over into every moment of your guests' stay. Messages can be beautifully lettered on plain mylar balloons.

As mentioned in THE SPACE, Chapter 7, balloons in bunches or columns can be used as dividers or backdrops that will make a large room seem smaller.

If you are trying to achieve the effect of small game booths at a carnival you can make mini balloon (helium filled) arches over a six foot table (attached on each end of the table) draped with brightly colored plastic or fabric cloths. If you have a flexible arch frame you can use air filled balloons intertwined with lights for a very bright and light effect.

Try using a centerpiece that can be easily carried out, so you can extend the life of the party by giving your lovely table decorations to guests to take home.

I wish to thank Meg Tuthill and Nancy Kruse (Tim, too) and Midge Docken who have helped me look good on many occasions. Through watching them in action I know a little bit about balloons and all of the wonderful things that you can accomplish with them. They are the Minneapolis M.O.B. (Mavens of Balloons).

Floral Arrangements

This is an area that I have, for some reason, never gotten too involved in and for that reason I know very little about. There are so many dozens of books available that give you wonderful and whimsical arrangement and display ideas for flowers sitting on tables, pedestals, shelves, hanging from the ceiling or in pots placed all over the event site. My expert advice in this category is to call upon your favorite (or your best friend's favorite) florist. Rely upon references to select the floral designer for your event. They are, as experts in most other categories, available in a variety of price ranges and levels of sophistication. Shop for your perfect match and you will be delighted with the results. The effects that a professional florist can achieve are almost beyond description.

Signs and Banners

In addition to the traditional practice of hanging signs and banners on walls to decorate and raise the spirits of the celebrating masses, it is now possible to rent the sides of buildings, buses, hot air balloons, and billboards to express your greeting.

I have covered the use of signage for directional help in event planning as well as for labeling areas of the event site. (See GUEST COMFORT, Chapter 12)

Some of the sign and banner ideas that I have encountered in my event travels are suitable for celebrations and some are more for promotional purposes. I will share them with you and hope that you don't get "hung up (I'm just having a little fun.) on deciding which is which.

Neon signs are wonderful for your front window, to greet your guests or to let the neighbors know that there is a celebration in your home. There are rental companies that offer neon signs such as: "It's a Boy," "It's a Girl", "Welcome Home", "Congratulations", etc. They rent them by the day or week.

Where to find: Signs or Neon Signs, in the Yellow Pages.

Lit-up marquee-type roadside signs are ideal to park on your front lawn or in your driveway to greet your guests for a special event. They are usually used to announce grand openings and sales but the rental fee is low enough to make them a feasible for special events, too.

Custom banners made of nylon fabrics are often works of art, when made of appliqued puff sculpture, and customized with your greeting, logo, name or design. You may pay considerably more for it, considering that it is for one event, but it will be useful for many years if you keep the greeting generic. These beautiful art pieces, if designed with reuse in mind, will be perfect for celebration after celebration. Some folks I know hang theirs out on their garage roof ritually to air their "festive announcements" on each family member's birthday.

If you need signs to make your event run more smoothly or to provide fun and entertainment, have them made by a professional signmaker or desktop publishing method. Poorly lettered signage is a "sign" of an unimportant event. I don't mean to be hard on you, but that is the truth. Be creative and innovative enough to find someone that will help you with signs, if your budget doesn't allow paying for them.

Notes & Numbers

Notes & Numbers

LIGHTS, CAMERA, INTERACTIONS

Since a photo is supposedly worth thousands of words and I have sprinkled the contents of this chapter throughout the book, I am submitting the following for this space:

~Chapter~

MEMORIES, WISHES & BLESSINGS

The nice thing about people these days is that they love those "good old days." We are in an era of "eras"... where nostalgia prevails at both business functions and at private and personal celebrations. When most of us look back on our lives we can enjoy more than a few good laughs. Weddings, anniversaries, birthdays and births, bar/bat mitzvahs, graduations and retirements, going away or coming home parties are all subject to a "tissue" grade (1, 2, 3 or "flash flood"). We love to laugh and cry ..(well, some of us like to cry) and both are good for a lot of things that ail us... (or so "they" say) So don't hold back those flowing emotions when you get the chance to let them go.

This little chapter is devoted to putting sentimentality; into rituals, ceremonies and presentations. So many times those special moments will come and go without being recognized or acknowledged. Now that's something to cry about!!!

Ways to Put Sentiment into Events

✳ In the invitation, alert the folks that they will get the opportunity to say a little something to the guest of honor on videotape. Suggest that they recall a memory or make a wish. This taped tribute will provide many years of enjoyment of these shared emotions and will be a great source of entertainment for future parties. If certain guests aren't good at public speaking or being "video stars" have someone else read their wishes aloud.

✳ Tender little wishes written by the guests to the honoree are tucked into helium balloons. If you have younger children as guests they can pop the balloons and read the greetings as a part of the ceremony.

✳ At a memorial ceremony a very touching moment is created when some of those wish-filled balloons are released to float slowly to the heavens. Most tender feelings of grief are so much easier to bear while in the company of those who share them.

✳ At bridal events everyone seems to love baby pictures or films of the bride and groom and their respective families. It is a sweet and foolproof way of embarrassing the happy couple while introducing the other guests to a little in-law history. A video presentation incorporating photos, video, slides and special graphics set to music is bound to create a wonderful, lasting store of memories.

✱ Poems, songs or skits that tell a *"This is Your Life"* story usually will get to the "soft core" of things. Everybody sings along or reads a stanza or plays a part. (Even if the part that they play is a non-speaking role . . . like an oak tree.) You can have these personalized presentations written by a professional or recruit one of your talented friends or relatives to write it. Again, be sure to video tape this valuable performance.

✱ Tape record the message of those not able to attend (You can tape it over the phone) and play it at the party. You will create a special feeling of closeness when you bring the voice and words congratulations of an absent loved one into the event. (Even if it is only a recorded message.)

✱ Wedding ceremonies are already comprised entirely of sentiment but there are ways to add even more. Couples are adding their personal touch by writing their own vows. Parents are renewing their vows at their childrens' weddings. I saw a loving bride and groom devote a special part of their wedding ceremony to presenting a lovely red rose along with a kiss to their mothers, grandmothers, and sisters.

✳ A lovely sentimental gift for new parents from their parents is a collection of photos and mementos from their babyhood. It is always fun to compare those photos with the new born babe to establish "who he/she takes after".

✳ You can give guests a chance to propose a toasts without them having to stand and speak. Place a small pencil and a slip of paper (printed with a graphic of two champagne glasses "clinking") at each person's place. Encourage everyone to write a personal message or wish to the guests of honor. These toasts are then collected and some are randomly read to the audience by an emcee. This type of presentation precludes the long, drawn-out program and allows even the most timid to propose a toast! (The little notes will make a great scrapbook addition.)

✳ Some lovely friends of mine were celebrating their 50th wedding anniversary and instead of gifts, they requested that each guest bring them a silk flower. As the guests entered, they placed their gift flower, tagged with their name, in a gorgeous mammoth crystal vase. It made a splendid display of love and beauty. The happy couple said that each friend present had contributed to the beauty of their lives as a couple, just like a growing and wonderful flower.

✷ A very sensitive and memorable way to pay a
tribute to a guest of honor is to publish a book
about them compiled of stories told by their
nearest and dearest people. Each guest submits
a significant experience or thought presented
either on paper or tape. The entire collection is
printed, as a booklet for all to have for their
own. The master copy is printed and bound as a
best seller and presented to the honoree.

✷ An elegant gift for a sentimental occasion is a
sterling silver tray engraved with the names of
all of the guests. The artistically arranged
names make a loving and creative design.

✷ My most memorable and touching sentimental
moment was a sing-along that took place at my
Dad's memorial service. He and Mom had a
favorite song which was ironically,
"Sentimental Journey." We provided printed
song sheets for everyone and had one of the
best song fests ever. We used lots of music in
the service because our family is musical. A
touching slide presentation was sweetly
accompanied by Kenny Rogers' "Through the
Years." Music can always pluck the heart
strings and for a few special moments
synchronize the beat of everyones drummer.

As this chapter quietly and sincerely comes to a
close I would like to suggest that when you have
the opportunity to express positive and warm
feelings to your loved ones take it and savor it. Not
meaning to get too philosophical, but we, as a
society, never seem to miss a chance to complain or

criticize even though praise goes a lot further in building close relationships. Write it, say it, play it, sing it, wing it or act it out. Do whatever feels right to you. Maybe it is just a pat or a hug. Give it!

Notes & Numbers

~*Chapter*~

18

Holiday Helpers

DON'T WORRY...BE HAPPIER

'Tis the season! and the arrival of the holidays mean it's time for gathering together for gift giving, sharing, caring and reminiscing. Sounds like fun, doesn't it? Well, it can be not only fun, but friendly, festive and trouble-free if you try some of the ideas in this chapter. Tasks, of all degrees of importance or effort, can be performed with ease if they are planned, prioritized, scheduled, and (here's the big one) *shared*.

> **Serve potluck style**, inviting guests to each bring one specialty dish. Ask them to share their recipes which you can print as a collection to be included in an after-holiday note along with a photo or two taken at the

gathering. The potluck plan saves the effort spent on the actual event which can be used for the after-event work of printing and mailing. the photos and recipes. The latter project is a more lasting and meaningful use of energy on your part.

Practice the two party system by entertaining two nights in a row. Cooking, cleaning, decorations, rental of equipment and, in some cases, entertainment, will be just a little more extensive and/or expensive for two days than for one. The bonus is that your home will be in an uproar for only one week of PPS (Pre-Party Syndrome).

Set up special space and plan activities for kids. Recruit an older child, from one of your guests' or neighbors' families to oversee your younger visitors. It will give the adults a chance to enjoy each others company and you can relax a bit knowing that the kids are occupied. Have toys and games on hand, rent popular videos, serve special kid's fare and decorate the area especially for the children.

Vary and simplify your holiday entertaining by giving a light brunch or dessert party. You can still see your favorite people and exchange gifts, but by sharing simpler food and beverage you are creating less work for yourself.

Invite a group for a cookie or candy exchange or a gift wrapping session. Some of the traditional holiday trappings (good word for them) have lost their luster and the work of getting them together can border on drudgery. But, performing holiday tasks while socializing can be an excellent excuse for festivities! Serve gourmet coffees, teas, or sparkling punch to the crew as they create their masterpieces. When your gang is all done with their "chores" treat them to a light snack or dessert.

Decorating your home for the holidays can be the theme of a party. Bring out the lights, trimmings and special decorations and set up a crafty table for the artists to create new decorations. Serve a casual meal or light snack along with some favorite holiday beverages. Have a contest for the best displays, ornaments or artistic endeavor.

Hard to Find Gifts: Here's a suggestion to help you if you are having trouble finding that special gift for a certain someone on your list. Shop for several small items that fall into one category such as photography equipment, needlework items, fishing paraphernalia. Wrap each one individually, then make up one large package for a personal and most thoughtful gift. A few of these small items combined with a gift certificate to that specific shop is also very creative.

Avoid giving the gift certificate-in-an-envelope only. That is far too impersonal. Always include a small token gift that compliments the certificate, as mentioned previously. Other examples: Wrap a dinner certificate with a small box of after dinner mints, a pack of elegant cookies or a miniature bottle of liqueur.

Do your shopping at certain times to avoid crowds. Gift shopping will be less stressful if you avoid the crowd by going very early in the morning or during dinner time. If you go in the morning you'll find that the merchandise is freshly arranged and the stock is ample. Aside from the smaller crowds there is no particular perk to shopping at dinner time, other than possibly losing an ounce or two if you skip dinner. The last suggested time to shop, where you will avoid crowds is July! A little picked over, but.......

Send postcard greetings. Postcard greetings are easy and quick to write, economical in price and have been proven to be read more often and more promptly than traditional cards. Photocards make a double impact since today's photo is worth a hundred (or is it a thousand?) words. [Ed: Is that edited or unedited?]

Idea: Recycle a used greeting card by turning it into a post card. Cut the front from the back and write your message and the address on the blank side of the picture section. To have some holiday "ha ha's" send this card back to the original senders...just to see if they are paying attention.

✳ **Cover some of your furniture for the holidays.** Take some anxiety out of your entertaining by covering light covered or fragile furniture with colorful holiday fabric throws,and replacing decorator breakables with holiday objets d'art.

✳ **Purchase a stain remover kit** that deals with wax, wine, food and other heavy traffic soil and you will be prepared for any holiday entertaining staining.

✳ **Give your pets a holiday gift!** If your pets are not "guest proof" (especially when little children are going to be around) do yourself and the pets a big favor and let them stay with a neighbor or in a familiar kennel for the day of the party or weekend of the event. You won't need to worry about them being "kidhandled", nipping at someone in the excitement or accidentally escaping and getting lost.

✳ **Give yourself a gift and get help!** Secure needed equipment, shopping resources and references from your friends or family. You will not only save money and time but avoid adding more stress. Reinventing the wheel is a thankless and meaningless task that is also filled with stress.

✳ **Consider hiring a professional planner** or an assistant. (See PARTY PLANNERS, Chapter 25)

Having someone to do your detail work will result in you pulling off an enjoyable and relaxed event. Professional planners will save you time and money by knowing just where to find things and at the best prices. If you have a full time job, this may take all of the pressure out of holiday entertaining. Hiring a school teacher or college student who is on vacation at this time could work perfectly and be quite economical.

Be sure to read PARTY POOLING, Chapter 19 for ideas on how to make your holiday party even less work by sharing resources and labor with friends or neighbors.

~Chapter~

19

Party Pooling

PUNCHBOWLS TO PIANO PLAYERS

We join forces to drive our kids to school, we team up to baby-sit for each other, we pitch right in when it's painting or moving time. Farmers assist each other in "raising barns," "bringing in the crops," and as a community, continuously help each other to succeed.

This chapter is to introduce and promote an idea of mine: Party Pooling. This is the era of two-career families, parents and kids attending college at the same time which allows less leisure time. This, combined with the explosion of the celebration industry results in situations where we're living longer, celebrating more and having less time for preparing. It could take the fun out of partying but this chapter is all about a concept which could prevent that from happening.

With the creation of a Party Pool among your family, neighborhood, company, organization or friends' network, you can support and encourage the fine art of celebrating. By sharing talents, equipment, labor and resources, everyone wins. The benefits of having a "party pooling" membership can include saving time and money for almost every type of event. The time savings in just searching for party ingredients is worth the effort of creating and coordinating your pool.

SETTING IT UP

First of all, let it be known that someone has to take the initiative to put some time and energy into organizing the pool and recruiting the help to maintain it. There are three ways of running your pool.

1. Simply printing and distributing a directory for the members (fellow employees, relatives, neighbors, association members) to use arranging their own pooling.

2. More formally, printing a directory and setting up a record-keeping system that keeps track of "who-owes-what."

3. More elaborately, to Plan #2 add: using the Pool as a fundraiser. By charging rental prices on equipment and hourly wages for help and eventually putting the money into a fund.

(Takes a computer and person to maintain the records).

Okay, now that you've decided which plan you are going to follow, and you have established a group of participants it is time to gather information. Send a form to each participant that requests information as follows:

List talents that you are willing to share:

Singing, piano playing (a biggie), other musical abilities, dancing, acting or comedy, clowning, face painting, graphology or card reading, magic, mime, juggling....etc.

Calligraphy (also a biggie), artistic flair, any writing, creative crafts, cake decorating, sewing, costume design, graphic arts, photography and video, desktop publishing, athletic prowess, carpentry, electrical, etc.

List items that you are willing to share:

Furniture, serving ware, costumes, decorations, props, lights, signage, linens, tents, and any items that would otherwise have to be rented.

Note: Decorations and props that have been created for special events that are too good to throw away, but not easy to sell are frequently stored in basements or storage bins Be sure to inquire about these sorts of things. They have great value!

List vehicles that you are willing to share: Vans, trailers, buses, classic cars, boats, bikes, wagons (horses, too), amusement-type rides, sleds and snowmobiles. (Can't forget the snow bunnies...)

List services that you are willing to perform: Typing, word processing, collating, general office, addressing, telephoning, errands, P.R. services, soliciting prizes, printing, researching, make-up, hairstyling, gift wrapping, shopping, bartending, serving and catering, baby sitting, pet sitting, host/hostessing, registration, coat checking.

List labor that you are willing to do: Preparing a yard for guests, cleaning (before or after), picking up at party, putting up decorations such as balloons and banners, decorating tables, etc., supervising other help, valet parking, chauffeuring guests.

List limitations or preferences: For instance, no Sundays, no daytime events, no alcohol or smoking, no outdoors events (allergies); and so on.

Rule of thumb: If members are willing to share a skill or talent that is their actual line of work, their commitment (per time) should be limited to an hour or two. The best use of this "experts" time would probably be in training someone else to perform the task.

A complete list of estimated values for services rendered or items used could be included in the directory so that members have an idea of what savings they are making or how much Pool-time they are using. Put an hourly rate on services and an actual rental fee on equipment. You will probably add more to your application that is pertinent to your locale or your groups' special interests.

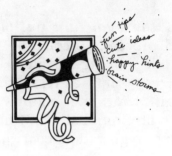

Important: Try to get the kids involved, too. The talents and the abilities of teenagers is incredible...not to mention their energy and enthusiasm. Your invitation, poster or program could be the result of an art or photography student's class project. Perhaps, he/she could be graded on it for extra credit. If you can pay them, it is a great way for kids to earn extra money, while developing special talents, know-how and gaining valuable experience.

When you have all of your forms completed, the information verified and listed in the official directory congratulations! you are a Party Pool. Only members will have access to the directory, (unless you are in Plan #3 and want the additional exposure to pump up the funds.) Once the directories have been printed and distributed, "Let the parties begin!"

In Plan #1, making arrangements to utilize each other's "stuff and skills" is up to the individuals. No record will be kept of the activity; it would be up to each member to keep track of his/her own participation and of course, say "no" when necessary.

For Plan #3, in which you keep close records of who uses the services and how much time or money has been exchanged or earned a computer- friendly member will deposit into the Pool by setting up the system. Each "rental" of equipment or "hiring" of talent (always at reduced rates to be agreed upon by the group) is entered, funds collected and deposited into a special interest-bearing account.

This plan is great for organizations, entire neighborhoods, companies, teams and schools or churches. Collecting the funds to support a trip, uniform or equipment purchase, awards banquet, or blow-out party makes sense for groups of all kinds. Employee bashes, picnics or outings will be literally free if the Pool has been set up to raise funds.

Example:

Member A uses Member B's punch bowl, tent, tables, chairs and banner. The total cost ,if rented from a service,would have been $500. The discounted Pool price is $100.00, which A pays into the fund. B gets credit for $100.00 worth of pooling and A gets a receipt which may or may not be tax deductible, depending on the fund.

Another Example:

Member B uses Member D as a piano player and agrees to pay $25 to the fund. The going rate would have been $100. Member D gets $50 credit toward future use of Pool services. This system serves to prevent any members from abusing the Pool, as sometimes, unfortunately may occur.

Party Pooling can expand your resources by immense proportions and with the great surge of energy and expertise that is involved, new attitudes towards entertaining can be born.

Now that you have a large and varied bank of equipment and services to dip into along with a huge team to help you stay afloat, go ahead and jump into the Party Pool— where you will never again get in over your head.

Notes & Numbers

~Chapter~

PENNY WISE PARTIES

I remember the trauma of going to a wedding and seeing the same people that would be attending my own wedding to be held just one week later. It was a mind-blowing extravaganza! A fantastic affair, with no "purse string" tightened. I estimated that the cost of the flowers on the tables alone was equal to what I would be spending on my entire wedding and reception. Well, that's life, and that's what makes event planning a challenge. I've always said that anyone can go out and spend money. It takes a real talent to stay within a budget creatively. I'm big on rationalizations! I never skimp on them. You will find them generously sprinkled throughout this book. Help yourself when you find the need.

This chapter is for the person with more time than money, since saving money is very time consuming. Searching and comparing (or, as I call it, "scrounging") takes lots of time; but, producing an elaborate event on a limited budget can be extremely rewarding.

Consider this: If you do not have lots of spare time (and most of us don't), find others to help—people who will find a challenge and see the fun in hunting for bargains. If you drive yourself crazy trying to save a few dollars, you will take a lot of the enjoyment and anticipation out of your party or wedding. Keep the value of your working or playing time in mind. For instance: If your wage is $10.00 per hour and you spend 3 hours running or phoning to save $15.00...you see what I mean.

O.K., you're still reading, so that must mean that you're going to work with me...Great!

The first step is to make a long list of friends, relatives or work mates that will volunteer their time and talents.

(See PARTY POOLING, Chapter 19)

Here are some basic money saving ideas for special occasion planning:

* Have the event in your own house, in your apartment building or condo party room, or anywhere that won't charge a fee. (Be careful though, that the cost of renting equipment doesn't offset the free room.)

* Most commercial party facilities have large quantities of equipment and supplies that may include decorations and props that, if used, could save you considerable amounts of money

❋ Bring in your own food and beverages.

❋ Recruit help for preparing food as well as setting up and serving.

❋ Shop around for suppliers that will sell to you in bulk at wholesale rates. Industrial sizes can be purchased at Wholesale Clubs that are very popular now. If you are planning to serve an item that you know is served in restaurants, you can probably purchase a quantity of that item through a wholesale distributor. Large quantities of items such as cheese, meats, fruits and vegetables can be purchased from farmers markets and wholesale distributers. If shopping at a discount food market, be sure to use coupons. Most locales have a wholesale bakery outlet that features day old items that if stored in the freezer, will be delicious when served at your event. This is especially true of rolls, danish, nutbreads and cookies.

❋ Scout around for tables and chairs that you can use or rent cheaply. Try your school, church or recreation senior center.

❋ If you do rent bulky items, don't scrimp on the delivery fee. It's usually only a few dollars and well worth the convenience.

❋ Rent your own helium tank and buy balloons from a party supplier to create simple decorations. The library will have books on working with helium and balloons, or you may have a (preferably adult) friend that has that special talent.

Suggestion: Hire professionals if you want elaborate balloon decorations, arches, columns and special

155

shapes. In the long run, you will save money and get long lasting, durable balloon displays that are just exactly what you want.

✳ Network to find your music and entertainment. There's always a friend or family member that is "in a band." You'd be surprised what you'll discover in this talent treasure trove. Make sure to take a look at them "in action" , though. The other option is a D.J. who will not only play music for every taste but conduct contests and mini-shows. The cost of a D.J. is somewhat less than live music.

✳ For fabulous decorations at frugal prices, call the display department of your local shopping mall or larger department stores. Check to see if they have any castoffs or rentable items. Because they rotate displays regularly they probably have quantities of usable decorations in storage. You can offer to donate a low rental fee to a charity in their name. Another good source for props is the high school or college drama department which might have some basic items for your event. To perk up the "previously used" items you can add fresh flowers (from the farmers' market) and balloons. (Check PLANNING RESOURCES, Chapter 29 for catalogs, props, decorations).

✳ If you want inexpensive original and custom invitations, decorations or posters, call the head of your high school art department and ask for help in recruiting some talent. You may also call aspiring young art directors or fashion designers who are studying at the local school of art and design. They can help you to create something wonderful, fresh and individual. (You could even make it a contest!)

✼ The technical college or vocational school in your town will have bakers, cooks, floral designers, seamstresses, printers, wait staff, lawn services, valet parkers, sound and light technicians. Students planning careers in various areas of the service industry are always looking for extra "earnings-while-learning." You will benefit from their energy, enthusiasm and excellent skills. They may even be able to get school credit for working on your project.

✼ Most every town has a discount paper/party store with competitive prices. The chains and franchises usually have lower prices because they buy in huge quantities. They have a wide variety of plastic and paper products for entertaining, household and office use. Most now have decorations, banners, balloons and related items. (Check to see if they give committee discounts.)

✼ For glassware, dishes, serving pieces and other food and beverage supplies, find a restaurant and bar supply company. They will sometimes work with you for a sizeable order. These purchases are smart, especially if you are starting a Party Pool.

✼ Rental companies often sell used items. It is a good way to pick up equipment and supplies for frequent entertaining. (Or that Party Pool)

Question: How many of you have worn your wedding gown, bridesmaids dress or elegant ball gown, for any other occasion? *(Raise your hands.)* Bridesmaids know the sixth biggest lie: "You'll be able to wear this hot pink silver lame trimmed number again..." My very practical suggestion for a bride or belle would be: find someone your size that has been a bride or ball goer in the past two years or so and make a deal to use her gown. If she is someone that is unknown to your friends and family, no one will have seen it and she will probably be thrilled that the dress will be worn again. You can save hundreds of dollars this way and take some anxiety out of your wedding event. I know of an extremely sensible bride that wore a recycled gown and allowed her bridesmaids to do the same. She then arranged a lake weekend for the "ladies-in-waiting" and paid for it with the savings. (Sometimes the "scrounging" isn't done to avoid spending money but to allow people to spend the money in more meaningful ways.)

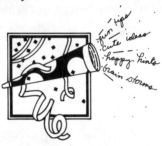

✳   Watch the ads for gowns "Worn for three hours" or "never worn". (I always wonder what the story behind that type of ad would be.) You can make some incredible buys. (And in some cases a new friend.) You will also notice ads for sample sales and wholesale gown bargains that are very worth investigating.

✳   Another old fashioned option for a bride is to find a relative who was married in another era and combine sentimentality and $$sensibility by using her gown. It is a romantic and special way of saving. Thrift stores, vintage clothing shops, (see RESOURCES, Chapter 29) consignment shops are all great places to find those unusual one-of-a-kind glamor garments.

✳ Don't forget the magical talents of a good dress-maker for alterations. The addition of decorations such as sequins, beads and trims of all kinds. By utilizing their artistic talents on a well-made basic gown, you could end up with a masterpiece.

Motto: The least expensive place to shop is in someone else's closet.

ONE PLACE NOT TO SAVE MONEY! Do not leave the documentation of your event, the result of which is priceless, in the hands of Uncle Joe or Cousin Charlie...unless that is what they do for a living. Trust me on this one! Hire a professional that is in the price range that you can afford. (There are variances in style, experience and cost.) In some cases you can pay a pro by the hour to snap the shots and have the film developed yourself. If you have a list of photos required all set up, plus and someone designated to assist by gathering all of the principles together for the photos, it will save on the hourly cost of the photographer. The same holds true for the videographer. The more organized you are, the less you will have to pay your cameraman.

Recap:

✳ Ask for help from talented and willing people.

✳ Keep in mind your hourly wage.

✳ Ask yourself: *"Will this purchase add to the fun?"* and *"Will anyone really notice...?"*

When it is a really tough decision about a purchase that I really have my heart set on, I stop and ask myself, *"If I amortize this purchase out over 50 years...let's see, that is $10.00 per year, less than $1.00 per month or 3 cents a day."* I

159

call it creative rationalization. It works for me.

I guess I'm just like Burger King...sometimes I just have to break the rules.

Notes & Numbers

~Chapter~

BENEFITS, BALLS & BALLGAMES

The experience of raising funds for your organization, a favorite charity or school/church can be rewarding, fun and exciting, but it is also very hard work. If you are involved in putting together a sizeable event, it can take hundreds of hands and even more hours. There is always a specific mission and most often is led by a seasoned board with a definite plan. The following tips are for fund raising events and will hopefully help planners reach their goals with less frustration and anxiety. (Planners: Investigate the 3 x 5 card system in THE PLAN, Chapter 3.)

Tip: When gathering a group to recruit volunteers for a fund raising project, provide seating for fewer people than you have invited. The psychological effect of having to bring in more chairs strongly suggests that there is a lot of interest in the project and creates an element of urgency. Empty chairs may tend to represent apathy.

The variable here is the number of people that you will actually have working on the project. No matter how many volunteers you start with, there never seems to be enough help when the zero hour arrives.

My rule of thumb: If you need forty "warm bodies" start with one hundred. Thirty will not show up, thirty will forget what they are supposed to do, and you will end up with forty. That may sound sarcastic or facetious on my part, but my experience tells me that the same "dirty dozen" make events happen. They will be the first on the site to set up, last to hop in the shower (if they get to do that much) and with seconds to spare, make a dramatic entrance (hair still wet) as the curtain rises on their big event.

The vital, high priority position of Volunteer Coordinator should be established to be the "banker" of all volunteers. Whenever a committee head needs help, he/she can call in to "the bank" with their request. It will be as quickly granted from this bank as from an employment agency. Unless volunteers have valid reasons for not appearing as promised, put them at the (very) back of the file for the next project. Organizations lose more wonderful committee heads by letting them down in the "help" department.

Suggestion: Utilize good volunteers with only an hour or two to commit, rather than overusing a few people that are willing to work for many hours. This encourages more people involvement, and, generally, the more people that are involved, the more tickets that will be sold. The new blood will add energy and give the hard core helpers a sense that they are not alone in their belief and commitment.

Your Invitation: In fund raising you must, I repeat, *must*, make an offer that cannot be refused. Your invitation must be designed to match the mood and theme of the event and it must stand out in some special way. **Don't scrimp here.** Follow-up phone calling is also very effective.

Tip: Tickler postcards reinforce the message. (You'll find tons of ideas in INVITATIONS, Chapter 10.).

Celebrity Participation: Always include the spouse or significant other of the celeb. I mean, actually invite the "wind beneath their wings" [Ed: What if they don't know the song?] to "flip pancakes," perform as a model, get bailed out of jail, or appear on a panel of judges. The "celebrities" will be more inclined to participate with the involvement of their "equal half" and from the spouse you will be likely to get some extra help and enthusiasm that the typical "limelighter" is too busy to give.

Selling Tickets: Don't rely on P.R. to sell tickets. Publicity will be instrumental in furthering awareness of the fund, giving the event credibility and reinforcing your invitation. But when it comes to actually selling tickets, it always comes down to friendly "arm bending." Try not to invest too much manpower, time or money into getting publicity—especially if you are short staffed. It's better to get energetic about selling lots of tickets.

Auction Items: As in P.R., the same goes for gathering items for silent auction tables. Well-meaning committee members will vigorously solicit manicures, haircuts, free meals and other items that may bring an auction price of much less than one ticket sale. The time spent in the multi-handling process of soliciting, picking up, ticketing, displaying, directory listing and collecting the money for these low price items is better spent selling tickets. All

"Under $25" prizes can and should be used as door prizes on raffle tickets. Some will disagree with me, but it's been proven that diluting the auction with ordinary or commonplace items detracts from the high bid items.

More About Auctions: The success of the auction will be seriously hampered if there aren't enough people there to get those bids up, up, up. Too few people and you lose that competitive feeling and sad to say, truly valuable prizes go for embarrassingly low amounts. When soliciting auction items, seek the unique and unusual items or services that normally cannot be purchased. Dates with celebrities or experts for lunch or dinner, television or radio appearances, customized products, exotic travel, original artworks, or special in-home services are all very desirable high ticket auction items.

Sponsorship: As a fund raising chair, keep your eyes open for restaurants or businesses of other kinds that are starting up in your community. Most likely they will have a grand opening celebration where a charitable tie-in would be very appropriate for it. The new business gets the benefit of your organizations support and not only will a portion of the sales or proceeds go into your fund but you can also realize some promotion and public awareness by being involved with the event.

Acknowledging Contributors: This gesture is very important towards creating a solid "patron" list. Give an accounting of the final result of the event, examples of how the funds will be used, and sincere expression of gratitude. The effort of showing gratitude is well spent and the reward is a stronger connection for the future fund raising. Here again, a postcard format is not only adequate, but recommended.

I heartily commend all of you who help others by creating and implementing fund raising events. You are part of an army with a wealth of brains, brawn and beauty...of the inner and outer quality. Some might wonder why each of us volunteers instead doesn't put in a month with an overload company and donate our wages to the fund? Money would probably be raised more easily that way. **(What? And give up show business?)**

A perfectly appropriate story written by Erma Bombeck, who has been the source of thousands of pleasurable moments for me, relates how we women go through all the craziness of putting on these fabulous fund raising events to raise $10,000. (I know. It has been lots more.) A man, however, can make a three-minute phone call, get a commitment for a few thousand, set a golf date and that's that!! But, men (poor souls) never experience the supreme thrill of dipping a thousand pounds of macaroni and a pound of feathers into red, white and blue paint and then, sparkling silver glitter to masterfully create a four foot high non-moveable, rarely reusable centerpiece for a 4th of July (or was it Bastille Day?) extravaganza. **Viva Volunteerism!**

~Chapter~
22
Buffet/Bars

HERE'S WHERE WE DRAW THE LINE

Buffet style service is a boon to entertaining whether the mood is casual or elegant.

Reasons for using this "help yourself" way:

* To conserve on space when seating is limited and guests will eat standing up or sitting on chairs or sofas.

* The seating is adequate and tables are set for sit-down dining but unlike normal sit-down service guests are given a wider selection of foods and the option to choose what appeals to them.

This chapter covers the basic (and very flexible) set of rules for successful buffet table serving and the embellishments and creative variations of buffet line etiquette.

Rules of Operation

✳ If you have over fifty guests your buffet should be served from both sides with identical service of the food from either side.

✳ Carvers or entree servers should be on the end, serving both sides.

✳ If you must set a buffet table against a wall another method of double serving requires assertive direction from staff or guest help to direct the guests to begin the line on both ends and finish in the center. Identical service from both ends is crucial.

✳ Utensils and napkins should be picked up last rather than being juggled while selecting food.

✳ If table seating is provided, utensils and napkins may be set out at each place along with glasses, cups and saucers.

✳ With large groups seated at tables, the tables should be numbered and called in turn by number two or three tables at a time so that the line is just a little longer than the buffet table. Guests can wait their turn while seated comfortably visiting and relaxing.

✳ Larger groups with a longer wait until their table is called should be graciously occupied with light snacks or appetizers placed on the table, family style.

✳ If a buffet is served to a group that will eat standing or "perching" on whatever seating is available, it is even more essential that the line move along rapidly.

✳ Two round tables, one with salads and relishes, the other with entree and vegetables, would provide an interesting and more convenient way of serving. By being able to serve themselves from all sides of the table your guests will feel less awkward and more sociable.

✳ In addition to this multi-table service it is cordial to pass extra food to allow persons seconds without standing in line again. Once guests have staked out a spot to enjoy their meals, they tend to stay put rather than going through the hassle of standing in line again. By passing food, you give your guests a chance to eat at their own pace and you avoid ending up with a lot of left-over food.

✳ If your guests will be standing and visiting while they are eating serve only food to be eaten with fingers or toothpicks. Avoid food that must be cut or very messy foods such as barbecued meats since they are very awkward to eat at crowded standing-room-only events.

Grazing

Another current form of serving buffet style, called grazing, invites guests to move from table to table and help themselves to all sorts of foods.

✳ This informal placement of foods around the event space is reminiscent of the food barn at the state fair when sampling and tasting and returning for more was part of the fun of eating.

✳ These stations can be elegantly decorated, roped off for a "traffic flow" and arranged to create a maze-like design.

Grazing Themes

The opportunity to decorate and garnish each of these tables in an individual style, is a way to dramatically show off creative abilities. Not only can you create a different mood or theme with each table, but you can carry out each of the themes on surrounding dining tables. Establish small sidewalk cafes of international flavor with costumed servers passing wines that fit the various cuisines. This is a very effective way of serving "around the world" (different ethnic foods) or different courses.

Hint: The serving plate with the notch or indentation for a stem glass or cup is absolutely the best party innovation since the folding chair. A person can eat food, carry a beverage and even hold a purse while using one of these handy little items. They are available in plastic of various degrees of permanence. Those made of heavier lucite or melamite are a good investment and will hop from party to party for a group of neighbors or family members or party poolers.

Belly Up to the Bar: (Beverage, Salad, Sandwich and Soup, Entree and Dessert Bars)

Lavish collections of food arrayed in serving trays, dishes and special containers constitute another tradition in "help yourself" food service. The many and varied ingredients of the specific meal course (salad, entree, dessert) are presented to encourage guests to use their

169

imaginations in creating concoctions. Being able to pile on all of the fixings for a giant taco, a huge anti pasto salad or a gastronomic chili dog is true bliss for a real "bar-pro". These "build your own" food bars are especially popular for luncheons and casual meal events. Some with more than a little flair are:

Potato Bar: Baked potatoes with dozens of toppings.

Pasta Bar: Noodles, Sauces, Sausages, Meat Balls, Italian condiments.

Fondue Bar: Skewered vegetables, meats and seafoods cooking in hot oil-filled fondue pots, with sauces and seasonings. For delicious desserts dip fresh fruits and cakes into melted dark and light chocolate. Garnish these with nuts, coconut and whipped cream. [Ed:Yummy!]

Crepes Bar: Freshly flipped crepes, with variety toppings to create entrees and desserts.

Peanut Butter Bar: Appetizers, sandwiches, desserts made with creamy, smooth and crunchy peanut butter and all of the popular accompaniments like jelly, bananas, marshmallow toppings and chocolate.

Pancake, Waffle & French Toast Bar: A Carbohydrate Spree for breakfast, brunch or lunch.

Burger & Brat Bar: All the trimmings, variety of buns, salads and relishes.

Ice Cream Sundae Bar: A complete "quite-a-few" flavors ice cream supply with all of the fantasy toppings will unite guests of all ages, in a veritable feast made only in dreams. (Remember to include ice water.)

Your imagination's limit is the only boundary for choosing containers for buffet and bar service. Depending on the mood or theme of the event, the serving dishes, utensils and actual meal carriers can be practically anything that will hold or contain food.

Here we go with some unique and captivating serving ideas:

For casual or rustic buffet service:

❊ Rough wicker or wooden baskets, barrels, buckets, bins, tin dishes, pans, boxes or crates.

❊ Suggested linens for this casual treatment are unfinished muslin, burlap, rough linen, corduroy or gingham checked cotton.

For vintage, Victorian or old-fashioned service:

❊ Antique crystal or china dishes, bowls, crocks and serving pieces.

❊ Use wash basins for fruit and the matching pitcher filled with wild flowers for a pleasant and lovely centerpiece. Mismatched pieces are quaint and effective in artistic arrangements.

❊ Painted wicker baskets with or without handles are perfect for rolls and breads.

❊ Odd china cups and saucers and one of a kind silver settings are also charming touches.

❊ Crocheted or antique lace cloths, doilies, embroidered and cross-stitched cloths or bedspreads and quilts make gorgeous table covers.

171

Contemporary and futuristic service:

✳ Use containers of chrome, brushed silver, onyx, lucite and acrylic. Shiny foil flower pots, cannister tins, baskets, coated boxes (square and round), wardrobe organizers for shoes, accessories and jewelry all prove very functional as serving pieces and accessories on a "futuristic" buffet.

✳ Ultra-modern mylar, and luminescent fabrics and papers provide a sleek background for the contemporary containers suggested above.

Theme-oriented buffet service:

✳ Serving ware of all one color, substance or texture is another effective way to present a buffet. Copper, brass, crystal, china, silver, stainlesssteel, wooden baskets, colored plastic, acrylic, clay, painted tins, ceramic, wood, teak, metal baskets, onyxware would all create an interesting and attractive table.

✳ For an authentic Fifties party buffet how about a perfectly matched set of pyrex. (The taste of Sloppy Joes loses something if not served in Pyrex.) Cardboard baskets for burgers and fries and TV trays for efficiently separated courses can be really cool at a Jukebox Jamboree.

✳ Strands of beads, fringed tablecloths, feathers and satin ribbons would make a flapper flip! Roaring twenties buffet tables would not be complete without "anonymous" coffee cups for the bathtub gin or a violin case holding "hot" silverware.

Open House Buffet:

When ordering and preparing for an open house buffet, you can use the following rule of thumb for amounts of food you will need to serve a typical 5-7:30 "right after work" crowd of fifty people.

✻   Fifty drop-in guests will consume one cheese and cracker tray, one veggie tray and one fruit tray.

✻   Three hot appetizers and two cold should be allotted for each person.

✻   Cake or dessert will be eaten by only 30 of the 50 guests.

✻   If you are serving seafood, such as shrimp or crab, be prepared for your guests to consume 3-5 pieces each.

✻   Remember to provide a non-fish item for those guests that might be allergic to fish. Tortellini kabobs or chicken nuggets would be good choices.

✻   Coffee doesn't go very fast (even in the wintertime) but punch, designer waters and soft drinks do.

✻   Wine, beer and liquor will increase appetites somewhat.

✻   Dry snacks placed about on ledges, tables and counters will be convenient for guests who don't want to make an extra trip to the buffet.

✻   Greeting guests with cups of punch is gracious and accommodating and will ease the awkwardness of those moments when they first arrive.

Hint: If you are passing hors douevres allow at least three cocktail sized napkins for each guest and use larger luncheon sized napkins if you are serving "barbecued anything".

Hint: Don't forget the tidynaps! Have servers offer them to guests from their trays.

Another Hint: If you do not have staff for cleaning-up-as-you-go, be sure you provide sufficient waste baskets or garbage receptacles for disposable plates and utensils, especially near the buffet table. People have a tendency to bring soiled dishes back to the table. if they don't find trash containers. These receptacles should be attractive and spotless.

Note: For leftover food: Individual sized see-through take-out containers can be filled with food, and set out for the guests to take home. Guests are shy about filling the "go cartons" themselves but readily accept them from the host. Restaurants or hotel banquet rooms will not pack large quantities of food for a host to carry out, but individuals can take small portions, as doggie bags.

Open house receptions typically feature fruit and veggie trays, cheese and crackers, and hot and cold appetizers. These light and fresh items are perfect to hand out to departing guests for a little post-party snack. Cakes and sweets are a delicious departing gift, too.

Request that your sales and catering director make these containers available to you. If you are entertaining at your home or place of work you can purchase these containers at your local deli supply store. If you need a small amount (fifty or so) your supermarket deli may sell them to you.

Warning: Donating leftover cakes and sweet dessert items to seniors citizens or kids, though generous, is not a good idea because eating sugar rich foods is not encouraged. Give them fresh fruits and vegetables and more wholesome foods instead.

Possible Buffet Line Pitfalls:

A long and slow-moving line, especially at a wedding where the guests have just spent considerable time standing in the receiving line calls for a few unorthodox procedures. I suggest seating the guests at tables and calling tables by number for the receiving line, if you anticipate a long buffet line. Serving champagne and light snacks to guests who are either standing or sitting at tables while waiting to get into the receiving line is very cordial. (It is imperative to seat older or handicapped guests if you cannot move them to the front of the line.)

If your event is being held in a very large room, place the buffet table near the dining tables. Then strategically place dividers or plants behind it to create a faux wall that gives a more intimate feeling. Many guests may feel awkward standing in a buffet line that is "up in front" of the room and the crowd. Placing the table off to the side is another way of creating graceful serving.

175

Hint: If you have carefully planned your buffet meal with a limited number of main entree portions, it is important that you have a server to monitor the amounts taken during the first pass through the line. This prevents the possibility that several guests with hearty appetites may help themselves to the extent that you run out of your entree before everyone has been served. (The Party Givers Nightmare) After everyone has their first helping it is not necessary to monitor.

The Potluck Pizza Party: Invite a gang over to bake their own pizza. Each guest will be a "Chef Boyardeelicious" when they bring the toppings of their choice and the hosts provide the crust, servingware and beverages. The invitation that was sent included paper chef hats, name tags, streamers, noisemaker and balloon. The Pizza Party Pack including instructions were sent in a 10" pizza carton. The excitement and "fun-having" started for the hosts when they dropped those invites into the mail. The guests, however, had to wait until they received them.

Garbage Can Dinner: It is cooked in and served from a huge galvanized garbage can. As you may have noticed, I am not into recipes. This will be the only recipe that I include in this book but it is more of an event than a recipe.

Invite 100 of your nearest and dearest friends over for a "Can-luck" dinner. Actually you can divide this recipe and invite any amount of guests. I will be giving you a per person recipe.

Place a case of beer (24 cans opened and standing upright) in the bottom of the can as a base for the vegetables. Cut cabbage in quarters and place on top of the beer cans. Scrub red potatoes and layer them, skin on, on top of the cabbage. The next layer will be onions cut into quarters (skin off) and scrubbed carrots cut into large pieces. The crowning glory of this delicacy is a variety of Bratwurst sausages resting on top of the works. The spices are caraway seeds, salt and pepper. (Use as desired) The can is now ready to be placed on top of a charcoal fire, surrounded with rocks to hold it from the fire, for about two hours. The steam from the beer and the juices from the vegetables and meat mix, soak, and permeate the solids to provide a wonderful hearty meal for the waiting crowd. The chopping, cutting and cooking turned out to be fun for the whole gang at this outdoor casual event. When the food was ready it was removed, layer by layer from the garbage can and laid out on trays for serving. A little butter was drizzled over the vegetables by those who wanted to add a little guilt to this healthy meal.

The suggested amounts of food for each person are:

Two potatoes, two carrots, one half onion, quarter head of cabbage, two brats. (The meal can be prepared for fifty in a smaller can)

Another reason I included this party idea is because it somewhat depicts my cake theory. Layers and layers, special fillings, delicious topping, seasonings, baked over a fire and enjoyed by it's many bakers. It is truly a casual buffet.

I thank Judy Gleason for this idea and recipe. She will serve it at her 50th Birthday Bash...(the kind of person that Judy is, a real party pro and a good friend to all, I wouldn't be surprised if she needs to use three garbage cans.)

(Note from the author: In my next book I intend to cover the art of "buffet line layering", the creative placement of food on a plate designed to hold one fourth the amount that you've taken. It is a true art and for only the most advanced party animal. I am afraid that you are not ready for it yet, it's very 90's. Watch for it, soon!)

Seriously, now, I hope that you will use this chapter and get in line for some beautiful and relaxed meals served "help-yourself" buffet style. (Wasn't the Scandinavian Smorgasboard the first buffet.?) [Ed: You betcha!]

Notes & Numbers

~Chapter~

FUN IN YOUR FUTURE

This new decade will see changes in the special event celebration industry that will reflect sensitivity, ecology, understatement and naturalness. Only glitzy extravaganza themes like Hollywood Premier, Lifestyles of the Rich and Famous or Millionaires Madness will call for the overly lavish and most elaborate details. Rather, the concepts of recycling, health, well being and relationships will permeate our special occasions. Sentiment and emotion have always been a very important part of most personal celebrations such as weddings, anniversaries, birthdays, and bar/bat mitzvahs or graduations. The dawn of the decade will encourage demonstrating our gratitude and pride at more peripheral celebrations, such as retirements, promotions, company employee functions and customer appreciation events. Attire will be more casual to match the casualness of food, service, atmosphere and decor. Entertainment will also tend toward the more personal and customized, including active participation of the guests wherever possible.

The Decor: It will tend towards more modest and simple design using fabrics and materials that are more natural, such as paper, cardboard, inexpensive fabrics and common flowers and plants. Balloons will fly as high as ever and elaborately designed arches, columns and shapes will provide the "bright and light" for occasions of all purposes. This inexpensive and voluminous method of filling spaces has been used for years and still represents celebration and festivity. The colors, patterns and shapes are myriad and ever expanding [Ed: Puh—leez!] (What can I say, those just slip out!) and really are appropriate for most any special occasion. Elegant and formal affairs will be enhanced by simple candlelight and down-to-earth floral arrangements set upon linens of any color or pattern. The drama will be added with color and texture rather than far out and fantastical displays.

Activities: 90's gatherings will be focused around adventure, with people stepping out of their own shoes for learning or testing themselves. There isn't a soul alive who doesn't love to face a test of skills, whether it's one of athletic prowess, intelligence or talents. Humor and sentiment, as I have mentioned, will be incorporated into personal, business or civic events. Taking guests to new locations, treating them to unusual or unique cuisine, customs and decor, or introducing them to an entirely new way of thinking or behaving are all situations that will prevail. By exposing people to new ways, products and ideas through social events we create an immediate bond of shared experience. This is the partial goal of most business and association meetings or conventions and all personal events.

Attire: The attire for the next decade's soirees will be less formal on the whole, because more casual entertaining will naturally encourage more casual dress. Picnics, barbecues, boat parties, hoe downs and costume events will increase the percentage of attendance because people with heavy work schedules who must wear suits or uniforms find casual dressing for recreation and social events appealing. Feather boas, sequin and bead covered gowns for the ladies as well as mens' patent leather pumps and tuxedos will be worn only for the most formal occasions. This laid back and casual trend may be more popular with the over thirty crowd, since the younger set is still very tuned in to glamour and glitz. So, tuxedo shop owners need not despair.

Food and Beverage Presentation: Refreshments will also be less formal with potluck and buffet style being the norm. In a typical two-career household the task of merely putting the event together, from invitation to cleanup, is a big job. Guests are glad to help out with either food or supplies, since they are fully aware of busy schedules and the limitations they impose on us. So, pitching in and making it a team effort is a good way to socialize more often, more easily.

Potluck How-to: The invitation is extended by the main hosts, each guest is assigned a component: Salad, Entree, Dessert, Activity. The hosts' responsibility is to provide the space, serving items, paper products, bread and rolls, condiments, ice and mixes. Setting a theme of: ethnic foods, all one color, all starting with a certain letter, all fast food, all homemade, all original recipes, all representing a state or city, (Boston Cream Pie, Texas Ribs, California Burgers, etc.) This takes a simple plan and adds a little challenge and surprise to it, turning an everyday potluck event into a production.

Idea for Potluck Guest: If the item you are providing can be delivered during the party, it will add an element of excitement and mystery. Or, if you are in charge of dessert, why not pile everybody into cars and take them out for an ice cream cone? By inviting a chef to whip up your particular part of the meal you will provide an entertaining highlight.

Sentimentality: There are so few opportunities to express our positive feelings for one another but 90's celebrations are going to encourage more of that through the presenting of meaningful tributes, videos, skits, gifts and spoken, written or recorded personal messages.

Adding the Sensory: The use of taste, sight, sound, touch, smell will be explored even further, as will the use of sentiment and humor. Slide presentations, videos, individual comments or speeches, roasts, musical tributes or ceremonies will appeal to all of the senses. Presenting a three act play for a guest of honor will not be out of line. The energy and thought that will go into these sensory-appealing performances will come back threefold in the appreciation and involvement of your guests. Some of the ideas for this show of affection will include:

❋ A "This is Your Life" presentation

❋ Skit or spoof on honorees work, life or hobbies

❋ Song(s) parodies either performed by soloists or sung by the entire audience.

❋ Game show skits such as Family Feud, Dating Game, Newlyweds, or Wheel of Fortune using only facts about the event's purpose in the game.

❋ "Battle of the Brains" Testing the audience on facts relating to the guest of honor or the event's purpose.

✳ A "We are the World" type video production, featuring all of the attendees. (This preparation will knock the socks off even the most sophisticated guest of honor.)

✳ "Man on the Street" video interviewing the honoree's hairdresser, tailor, boss, co-workers, relatives, (throw in a few total strangers for solid humor) pets, service men, teammates, etc.

✳ Comedian or actor doing a stand-up routine customized with all of the honoree's special information.

✳ A Real Roast. Make sure that everyone understands that they should start out by "burning" the roastee and then they can "cool down" and gently end their presentation with a warm and sincere toast.

Celebrities and Interesting Guests: The art of mixing various types of people for better events will be more customary in the 90's. Hosts will encourage guests to bring someone new and unknown to the group. The idea of enlarging our circle of friends and awareness will be enticing because most people will have such a limited amount of leisure time that their social and business invitations must promise pleasure and entertainment, along with relaxation and networking potential. (Have you heard about the laundromat/tavern/tanning booth/ meeting place?) Being forced to mix business with pleasure actually comes as a blessing because that's the way it is getting to "need" to be. To get the most out of a leisure hour, however spent, all of the elements (pleasure, entertainment, relaxation, networking and sensory) must be present. The ultimate challenge will be to make this all happen casually, simply and naturally.

Charitable Events: There will be a heavy push for charitable giving through sharing and caring events that will be designed with the intent of bettering communities, families and individuals. Events will celebrate and commemorate while benefiting others less fortunate. The trend toward conserving on the expense of entertaining to establish funds for worthy causes will grow more popular. Recycling information and educational programs will create an awareness and desire to avoid waste or overspending. More businesses and charities will collaborate in fund raising through event sponsorship and sales efforts hoping to encourage more people involvement. You will have the opportunity to give of yourself, your resources and your time while participating in fun and festivity.

Family Involvement: Projects and events that involve the whole family will be planned to allow parents and children to spend more of their quality leisure time together. The family reunion, picnic, outing and excursion will give more opportunity to bond and grow as a unit and as individuals while getting some R & R.

The Way It Will Be

So look forward to the 90's for events that have looks of natural and simple elegance the atmospheres of the 90's event are casual and relaxed the feelings of the 90's event are of sensitivity, adventure and health. Sounds pretty good to me. ***Let's Party Back To the Future!***

~Chapter~
24 Gift Giving

FOR PEOPLE WHO DESERVE EVERTHING

Most of the special events that take place in our lives require that a gift be given. Birthdays, anniversaries, weddings, showers, retirements, graduations and other personal celebrations call for a gift of some sort either practical, sentimental or downright silly. In most cases you will know the person or persons you are shopping for well enough to select a perfect gift. Often the honoree will be registered at a department store which makes it extremely convenient. Then you have the individual that is "that person who has everything" which poses a bigger challenge. This chapter is dedicated to gifts that are customized, unique and state-of-the-art as gift giving goes. They are available by mail or telephone order and on a national basis. Having fun in finding the perfect gift for a good friend or dear relative can be the beginning of the party for you.

185

Did I say State-of-the-art? Well how about up-to- the-minute?

Got A Minute? Want to buy one? *TimeKeepers* is selling deeds to any minute (not spoken for) that you request. You can commemorate the exact minute of birth, the minute you met, or any one of millions of specific sixty-second slots by purchasing it. The owner will receive an official deed for the minute that they own. For $20.00 you get an elegantly printed (in two colors) 8 1/2 x 14 inch "suitable for framing" certificate. Your document can be presented complete with a "time frame". Everyone has that special moment in time which may have changed their lives (or begun it) and now they can *own* it. 1-800-TICK TOC is the order number (you can use Visa/Mastercard.) So don't waste a minute and remember "There's no present like the time." (Say Hello to ..Don Stewart, a truly gifted and classy guy. He designed the cover of this book.)

If you have ever dreamed of being able to send a love letter that says just the right thing, romantically and artfully written on elegant paper to be cherished and savored forever? If so, you will love this product. *LoveLetters, Inc.* has a variety of perfectly worded messages for family, friends and significant others, elaborately calligraphied on your choice of high quality papers, sent in an attractive mailing tube, to your loved one. There is one for a bride to send to her parents which is especially meaningful and sentimental. The sympathy and condolence letters are perfect as a caring gesture. The cost for the basic letter is approximately $18.00 including shipping. You can call for their colorful catalog at 1-800-448-WORD. Invitations, announcements or customized letters can be ordered, too.

186

SongSendsations, Inc. will create a lively, loving and to-tally personalized song parody for a one-in-a-million gift item. You provide them with 15-20 pertinent facts about the honoree, including their favorite type of music and within days you will receive an audio tape of your song, recorded with fully orchestrated background music and sung by a professional vocalist. Along with the casette tape you will receive an attractive song sheet, your personal message or salutations printed with the custom lyrics. This sheet is packaged in a lucite box frame and shipped, with tape, to either you or your special gift recipient. If you wish, the song can be sung over the telephone and then sent on. A popular idea for presen-tation is to play it at the party (or in the office) and invite all of the guests to sing along to their own song sheet. The cost for "their own song" is $150.00 which includes shipping. Information can be obtained by calling 1-612-544-7441, ask for Roni.

A status gift for men or women who are career oriented, is the high quality wooden (with glass) "celebrity" frame. It features the business cards (matted attractively) of such formidable personalities as Thomas Edison, Abraham Lincoln, John Ford (you know—? Just the boys.) The female version features Amelia Earhart, Florence Nightingale, Betsy Ross and the like. There is a blank space for the business card of the recipient. You can send a check for $45.00 and you will receive the frame or if you send the business card, too, it will be gift wrapped and shipped to the "high achiever" of your choice. Send check and card if desired to: *S. Clein*, 4520 Excelsior Boulevard, Minneapolis, MN 55416, or to use Visa/MC, 1-612-920-7297. For graduations, new jobs, promotions or retire-ments this is the gift. (There are less expensive versions shown in mail order catalogs, but this one will do you proud.)

Big League Cards, Inc. will print up a batch of baseball cards (or whatever-sport card) for your special sport enthusiast. For an invitation, announcement, business card, or special favor use these colorful authentic-looking cards. The minimum order is 50 cards which cost $32.00 (100 are $42 and 1000 are $102) featuring personal information on the reverse side of the picture. Call Big League Cards for a brochure: 201-692-8228. Batter Up!

Picture yourself or a loved one on the cover of Success Magazine. For just $19.95 plus 3.00 postage and handling you can get this framed full color sensational gift. Send 3x5 or larger color photo to *Fotozines/Success*, P.O. Box 747, Windermere, Fl 32786. Include check or money order payable to Fotozines. Be sure to include your mailing address. (No P.O. Boxes.)

If the "everything" that your gift challenge has includes a poor memory for birth dates you can order a calendar personalized with up to 50 special dates to remember for only $9.95 It is available from *Artistic Greetings, Inc.* Dept. AG9-677, P.O. Box 996, Elmira, NY 14902. Just drop a note and they will send the order form. It would be an ideal gift for a busy grandparent. (My personal addition would be a batch of mailing labels, addressed to the family members.)

Dream trips, exotic expeditions, adventurous get-a-ways are all planned for you by *Outdoor Expeditions*. You can give that special someone an authentic safari, deep sea excursion, mountain climbing trek, or faraway foray. The entire trip is planned for you down to the last minute detail and the traveler need only show up with proper clothing and personal items. These unforgettable trips are truly gifts that will live forever through photos, stories and memories. Start your trip "dreaming" by calling Jay at 1-800-535-7850.

The International Star Registry will name a star for a special person in your life. This is a gift from the heavens. An embossed certificate, two charts noting where the star is and a booklet on stars comprises this galactical gift. A celebratory present for a couple is a pair of stars orbiting each other for eternity. They are both named and registered. Call for an application: 1-800-282-3333.

Several fine department stores feature custom gift services for both personal and business gift selection, one or one hundred at a time.(Discounts for volume purchases.) *Bullock's By Appointment* has a timesaving service that helps you choose ideal gifts for merit awards, company gifts and unusual tournament prizes. After assisting in the discovery of the perfect gift or premium items BBA will gift wrap and deliver them. After just a short visit with a professional consultant you can confidently "wrap up" your shopping mission. Contact the Bullock's store nearest you and ask for extension 444.

"Ah yes, you'll remember it well". Especially if you are reading your memoirs that, after an interview session conducted by *Robert E. Treacy, Ph.D.*, have been published for all time. You can use this highly specialized service for you and your family members to enjoy or present a gift certificate for the service to a loved one. The finished product can be published or recorded on cassette. Either one will be a treasured keepsake. Write or phone for information: Box 555, Bryn Mawr, CA 92318, (714)794-4300. You may also purchase a booklet that instructs you on how to do your own memoirs.

If you have a fishing enthusiast or novice, you can give him/her a fine fishing trip in Minnesota's favorite fishing lake region. It is especially popular with business executives but anyone will rise to the bait! (Ed: Give her the hook.) The anglers are picked up at 7 a.m. and "vanned" to the lake (continental breakfast on the way), outfitted with all gear, including license, rod and reel, bait and the boat. After an eventful (the fish are usually biting) day on the lake and a delicious rustic outdoor lunch of smoked turkey (not fish) the "happy hookers" are returned to their homes, hotel or office by dinner time where they can cook up their fish feast. Call Everett Williams, (612) 588-1211 or send for information and a *Fish For A Day* newsletter, 1409 Russell Avenue North, Dept. PS, Minneapolis, MN 55411.

Balloon Bouquets, anywhere in the country. Call 1-800-424-2323 and they will connect you with a reliable and reputable delivery service in your town (or the town to which you are sending your greeting .)

Anyone on your list that is a Disney Freak? You can obtain a jam-packed catalog of all Disney products that are popular and appropriate for kids of all ages (2-102) Send for it at *The Walt Disney Catalog, Inc.,* 3960 Willow Lake Boulevard, Memphis, TN 38118 You may have a Disney Store near you, they are all listed in the catalog.

Frame that Tune has designed a picture frame in chrome, brass and selected colors that can be used to frame record album covers. The beautiful art that adorned some of the classic albums can fill a den, office, recreation room or family room wall. Delightful childrens' record album covers, in pastel or primary colored frames make a delightful decorator statement in a kids room. Get those masterpieces out of the storage room and hang them up to enjoy, with easy to assemble and reasonably priced ($11.95-15.95) frames from Jackie Cameron, 6208 Wyman Avenue, Edina, MN 55436. Send for ordering information.

I have always been a greeting card maniac, spending hours in the card shops, hooting and howling over the wonderful and innovative cards that "those people" come up with. I have found lately that some of the cards are elegant, elaborate and a little expensive but in most cases are the gift itself. They are musical, pop-up, original art pieces, and come in sizes to fit anyone. Hallmark has cards and certificates that are personalized while you wait. One personal favorite is a Peanuts comic strip. When a gift is not in your budget, these cards will go a long way. (Especially if you put a stamp on them.)

Notes & Numbers

Notes & Numbers

~*Chapter*~

HASSLE-FREE HOSTING

After you have read through this book and undoubtedly have been inspired to throw a huge bash, you may be overwhelmed with the thought of all the responsibilities that are involved. Don't let that feeling slow you down. If you are pressed for time and low on ideas, consider calling an expert to help you get started. Whether you decide to hire someone to help you from "concept to cleanup" or just to consult in the creative planning stages, I guarantee that you will be glad that you did. The advice that a professional can offer will save you money and time (which is also money).

Taking advantage of a professional's knowledge of resources, costs and appropriate expenditures will give you a jump start and help you to avoid making mistakes.

Planners, whether they are independent or provided by a vendor (i.e. rental company, caterer, florist or decor designer), have several ways of charging for their services.

* *Hourly rate* for consultation ($25.00-$75.00) which should include a typed summary of the meeting, resource names, phone numbers, and a "guesstimate" budget for the items that were discussed. I compare this summary to a menu. You may expect to pay about $150.00 for this consultation.

* *The initial consultation fee* may be refunded if you hire him/her to continue on with the plan and implement the entire event. You will be charged an hourly rate or a percentage of your total event budget (usually 10-20%).

* *Commissions from vendors:* The planner will select and contract all of the vendors for the event and realize his or her fee from discounts given by the vendors.

* *Some vendors give complimentary planning assistance* and resource referrals, but they will not implement as the project progresses. Sales and catering departments of hotels, restaurants and banquet facilities will be very helpful in suggesting and reserving vendors for you.

Where to find planning assistance that is not professional.

* You may be able to recruit help from the local school of business, marketing, public relations or design for a non-paid internship or hourly rates ($5.00 to $7.00 per hour).

✳ Another source of planning help is a local nursing home or seniors' residence. The Special Activities director has experience and might welcome the opportunity to earn extra cash while doing a job that comes naturally.

✳ During the holidays, teachers and college students are on break so you may find help within that group.

✳ If your only need is for effective clerical and administrative help, hire an efficient temporary help or moonlighting employees.

Questions to ask when interviewing a planner.

✳ What is the planner's specialty? What type of event has he/she done most frequently?

✳ How does he/she charge? Hourly? By the Project?

✳ How many full time employees does the planner have?

✳ How long he/she has been in business.

✳ Does he/she do consulting by the hour.

❋ If the planner is doing your entire event will the planner be at your event or will he/she send an assistant?

In addition to asking the suggested questions it's also a smart idea to get the names of several clients for whom they have planned events that are similar to yours. *Important:* Give these people a call even though you know that they are going to give a favorable report.

The following organizations are the ones that most event planning professionals belong to. The phone numbers are listed so that you can give them a call if you would like to find the name of a member that lives and works in your town. It is a good way to find a reputable planner.

Association of Bridal Consultants

(203) 355-0464

International Special Events Society

(800) 334-4737

Meeting Planners International

(214) 746-5222

International Society of Meeting Planners

(602) 483-0000

American Institute of Floral Designers

(301) 752-3318

National Association of Balloon Artists.

(904) 354-7271.

National Association of Catering Execs.

(502) 583-3783

National Association of Reunion Planners

(407) 291-2941

Local or State Chamber of Commerce

Local Convention and Tourism Bureau

Where to Find: Professional event or party planners are listed in the Yellow Pages under Party Planning. Consulting with family and friends will also net you some valid suggestions and recommendations as will a call to your local party suppliers.

Tip: Once you have hired a planner, ask for weekly check-in-with-progress calls, but avoid excessive in-person meetings where the meter is running.

As a planner myself, I can't stress strongly enough the benefits of putting your utmost faith in your planner's skills and efficiency. I usually introduce my fee structure by saying, "If you trust me and let me go with my flow, you will get twice as much for your money." Even with restrictions most planners can produce more impressive parties than *almost* any lay person. As in any situation where you have hired experts, let them do what they do best. If you give them an opportunity to show their best stuff you'll get more than your moneys worth.

So ends my plea for professional event planners. In summation:

✳ You will get highly creative, professional and innovative event designing and planning from a well-respected and reputable professional planner for percentages or substantial fees.

✳ You will usually get knowledgeable advice and assistance from vendor-employed planners free or reasonably priced.

✳ Non-professional detailed administrative assistance may be all that you need to successfully implement your event.

No matter how busy you are you can have a successful event that is laden with details and special features. The secret is to get some help so that you can relax and enjoy your guests and your party. Have fun and don't forget to invite me. I want to come by and watch you being a guest at your own party.

Notes & Numbers

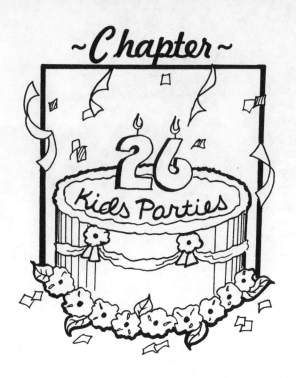

~ *Chapter* ~

26

Kids Parties

THEY'RE PARTY PEOPLE TOO

Kids parties are a highly challenging "whole 'nother thing" and take creativity, patience and most importantly, help. (Be sure to Party Pool this one every time.) It's the way most mothers become "party queens" in their own right. The challenge is even greater these days, with sophisticated television, movies, videos, print advertising and the worst culprit, peer pressure. It's work to find the answers to "What to do that will be fun, exciting, different, and keep the little darlings occupied?" It ain't easy.

"Children's parties" aren't my long suit (or long chapter) so I hope that the ideas I share with you can make things a little easier for you the next time you are faced with the "kids' party challenge."

Most under-five-year-olds' parties are usually more for the adults and older kids. In order to include everyone, though, we must come down to the common denominator which means all becoming little kids for a few hours. I frequently have to think of games for adults that will take them back to their childhood, when life was simpler. When they could occasionally get out of line and it would be appropriate—like at birthday parties. So the "everyone is a kid" party idea is to play childhood favorites: Pin the Tail, Musical Chairs, Fish Pond, Leap Frog and Relay Race. Children always love to see their parents acting silly and childish. Put kids and their parents on the same teams to make up an olympiad, awarding toy medals to the winning teammates.

The refreshments for this "kid-for-all" are easy, typical birthday party fare: cake, ice cream, sandwiches, soft drinks, tiny paper nut cups and other sweet treats. Mini-donuts, cocktail size wieners, cupcakes, miniature candy bars, animal crackers and sample size ice cream cones are all favorites of the tiny tots. They are easier for the little ones to eat and cute for the older "kids", too. Serving dishes, cups and utensils are available in small fry size, too. Serving the smallest children at coffee tables, mini-picnic tables or sitting on a plastic tablecloth for a picnic style meal will not only be novel but it will be more comfortable for the wee guests.

Kids costume parties are always fun. Some costume themes are Cartoon Characters, Zoo Animals, Favorite Book Characters, Occupations, or "Bring a Costume for Another to Wear." (Kids'll get real creative here, trying to contrive an embarrassing costume for another.) It's a good idea to give prizes to everyone for wearing a costume. (Polaroid photos for souvenirs).

Another costume idea is for everyone to wear old throw-away men's white shirts for a "paint n' sign" party. Start by giving each guest a set of pens and permission to decorate each other's shirts with personal designs or written messages. Some budding Picassos and Warhols will surely surface. Appropriate awards for outstanding artwork are art supplies, teen art posters or wild wear-able art in the form of T-shirts, hats or sneakers.

Colorful foods and beverages served on matching paper products will carry out the theme. Red Jello, orange juice, green peppers, white bread, grape jelly, black olives, etc.

Writing a short play, with costumes, props, and easy lines will give your young thespians a chance to show their dramatic stuff. Mom or Dad or an older sibling can be Cecil B. Shlemiel, (beret, director's chair and all). Video tape the performance and watch it right away. This is loads of laughs and gets everyone involved. Be sure to give the quieter types non-speaking roles such as trees, street signs or lights. Serve movie food like popcorn, soda, hotdogs and candy bars. Top it off with token trophy awards and a promise of a videotape of the production.

You'll get glowing compliments on an all neon party. The attire request is anything neon trimmed, the more the better. Balloons in bright neon colors are now available for glow-in-the-dark decorations. Glo-lite jewelry, bow-ties, glasses, and headgear can be ordered from the GTA catalog. (See RESOURCES, Chapter 29) that will make popular favors and prizes. Turn those lights down and let the glowing guests dance and prance in the black light. If you have the budget for a deejay, this could turn out to be the party of the year with the beat of today's music to the neon light show. Food and beverage will even glow if you trim the serving ware with neon paints (cups only) and tinsel hanging from the bottoms.

Taking children to other settings for a party is very popular these days. Some family restaurants feature party packages that are reasonable and with some special personal additions of your own, will work very well. The Zoo, museums, sports spots such as billiard rooms, bowling alleys, skating rinks, swimming pools and ski resorts have similar packages. (Video arcades are fun, but maybe kids do that too much on their own.) Teenagers love to go to a real nightclub atmosphere and dance up a storm to the deejay. This, combined with casual food, other lively activities make bar/bat mitzvah and sweet sixteen parties smashing successes.

Family Game Night: All members of the family will love a chance to compete with each other on a "board game marathon" night. Set up all sorts of popular games so that groups can play in several areas of the house. When the timer goes off the players count up their scores, tally them and move to the next area. It is like a tournament that can be organized by teams or as individuals. The spirits get high and the competition gets rough, but it is a great time for kids of all ages (including the 21-91 gang). Prizes or medal awards are presented, refreshments served and general fun is had by all.

For family picnics, company parties or group gatherings where parents and children are together for fun and games, be sure to plan games and events that provide an opportunity for all ages to participate. By organizing the group into teams (coded by colored hats, t-shirts, buttons or banners) you can keep track of the winners of each event and the winning team is the one with the most points. It is lively fun and a good chance for parents to interact with their children in a way that is not experienced very often in typical family situations. The same relay races, tug of war, sports games and games of skill can be played by all participants in teams made up of an equal amount of adults and children, and the scores will be balanced. Your families will end up winning, winded and plenty wound up after this active bonding experience. As in Family Game night, prizes and awards round out the event. (Kids seem to like the medals and trophies better than prizes.)

✳   Parties in a Bag has put together party kits for kids— a birthday party in a bag. Each kit parties eight kids and includes invitations, games, cake decorations, favors, party bags, thank you notes and step-by-step party guide complete with menu suggestions. Kits available are The Dinosaur Party, The Teddy Bear Party, and The Dectective Party. The prices work out to be about $3.00 per kid. (For ages 3-8) Send for information: Parties in A Bag, 14410 Orchard Road, Dept. PS, Minnetonka, MN 55345 or Call Carol: (612) 938-3477

I have helped to plan several great Bar/Bat Mitzvahs and always found it a challenge to find activities and enter-tainment that will keep the thirteen year olds occupied, even if it is an event that is "kids only". I have, however acquired a very good understanding of how these most important events work and what is neccesary to make them successful, from an activity standpoint. The in-formation is really a book in itself, or at least a healthy sized booklet. In order to do this subject justice I have written My Bar/Bat Mitzvah Activity Planning Guide which is available by mail by sending your name, address and check or money order for $5.00. You will receive a 50 page publication that is jam packed full of ideas and suggestions to make your bar/bat a huge success. If you aren't happy with it you can return it for a complete refund. The address appears on the ISBN page at the front of the book.

*"Everything But the Cake!" is a colorful catalog of kids party stuff. Send $2.00 to: 607 Corona Street, #272, Denver, Co 80218-3406.

Notes & Numbers

~*Chapter*~

RENTALS, CATERERS, SITES

This chapter features the advice of some experts in the fields of equipment rental, catering, sites, transportation and decorations. In the planning stages you will have the opportunity to ask for important advice of the suppliers that you may decide to use for your event. Asking the right questions is a key element in both selecting and working with your suppliers.

THE BANQUET SPACE INTERVIEW

Space that provides food and beverages.

✳   What are the current prices of meals and beverages, including all tips and taxes?

* What are the current prices of extra equipment and supplies?

* What are the dimensions of the space and it's suitability for all of your planned activities?

* What is the deposit and payment policy?

* What are the names and numbers of two customers who have held events similar to yours that you may call?

* Do they have handicapped access? A non-smoking policy?

* What is their food sampling policy?

* What is their cancellation policy?

* What is their food and beverage guarantee policy?

* Do they have a loading dock, elevator or move-in facility?

* What time will the room be available for setup and tear-down?

* What, if any, other events are being held in adjacent space at the time of your event? (especially, where only folding doors separate you.)

  Note: Important for wedding ceremonies and awards events that require a quiet atmosphere.

* What, if any, event will take place in the room just before or after your event? (There is the possibility that you may be able to share some decorations or equipment).

* What items are included in cost? (Room, staff, linens, candles, P.A. system, tables for gifts or registration, staging, lighting.)

* Are there adequate parking facilities? Free or pay?

* Is there a comparable event being held between now and your event date that you can look in on? (This can save you some serious mistakes.)

* What, if any, special rates on guest rooms or The Honeymoon Suite are available?

* What, if any, transportation is available to hotel guests?

Space that does not provide food and beverage:

Most of the above questions also pertain to this type of space but you will need the following additional information:

* Can you bring in your own food?

* If you are required to use a licensed caterer, may you select your own?

* What is the liquor policy? What is the corkage fee?

* What is the cleaning deposit?

* What is the deadline for cleaning up and removing equipment?

RENTAL EQUIPMENT SUPPLIER INTERVIEW

The following information has been provided by one of the finest rental equipment companies that I have the pleasure of working with in my town. They feature an elegant selection of rental equipment, linens, serving ware, decorations, props and also top-notch planning assistance. I called upon them for this list of questions for you to ask your rental expert. Thank you, *Charles M. Feldbaum, & Tom LaLiberte, Apres Party and Tent Rentals*, Minneapolis, Minnesota.

✳ What are the delivery and set-up charges?

✳ What are the terms of rental?

✳ How long can you keep the equipment for a one-day rental charge? Out by when, in by when?

✳ What is the condition and age of rental equipment?

✳ Will you get the same equipment as that shown to you?

✳ What happens if you lose or break an item?

✳ Does the equipment need to be cleaned before return?

✳ Are there any special charges for unusual places for loading and unloading?

✳ Will they bring along extra quantity or items in case you find the need for them and not charge you for them if you take them back? (extra tables, chairs, linens, lights, etc.)

✳ Will a supervisor be coming to assist in set-up or will it simply be delivered?

Additional Rental Tips

✳ Sometimes it costs the same to rent silver and china as it does to purchase fine disposables.

✳ Do not put soiled linens in closed plastic bags for return, they might mildew.

✳ If you are renting large quantities of tables, chairs, etc. you will need a volunteer crew to help set it up. The rental people can move just so fast.

✳ Move cars away from loading areas before the rental truck arrives.

✳ Assign someone to count items at the end of your event. Give a checklist to your sales and catering person. If any items are missing, it is possible that the banquet space will be responsible for them.

✳ Do not empty trash before all silver and serving pieces are accounted for.

THE CATERER INTERVIEW

Every catering company has a style and personality of it's own. The following are questions to ask a catering company to determine if they will be suitable for your special event. I thank my friend and associate, *Chuck Duberstein, Chuckwagon Catering, Minneapolis, Minnesota* for his help with this list.

✳ What are the portions and quality of food used?

✳ What equipment do they supply and what will you have to rent?

✳ Is there any discount if you provide all or any of the equipment yourself?

✳ What is the quality of linens, dishes, silver and glassware?

✳ What is their guarantee policy? Percentage of overage allowed?

✳ Will they guarantee their regular staff? (Not over-load staff.)

✳ Can they also provide complete bar service?

✳ How old is the serving equipment that they will use?

✳ Will they provide you with a written estimate of the menu with a breakdown of all costs?

✳ What extras to they have? (Flowers, candles, decor items, props, lights.)

✳ Have they ever catered in your event site?

✳ Will they provide you with a few references from customers that have had events similar to yours?

✳ Is all of the food prepared by them? (It might not matter to you, but it is good to know?)

✳ Will they allow you to serve food from other sources?

✳ Can they show you photos of events that they have catered?

212

Additional Catering Tips:

❊ Get three estimates to make sure that you have the best choice for your event.

❊ A prompt, professionally presented estimate is a very good sign of an A-1 caterer.

❊ Most caterers have great resources for things that you need for your event. In most cases, these refer-rals will be from first hand knowledge of people that they have worked with on other events.

❊ Ask your caterer to bring see-through "take-home" containers so that you can offer your guests a "care package" to take home, in the event that you have lots of leftover food. Especially good for fresh fruits and vegetables that perish quickly.

❊ Most caterers will whip up family recipes and con-sult restaurants or other caterers for recipes that you would like to include on your menu.

❊ Let your caterer do his/her thing, feature his/her specialty on your menu. You will get wonderful variety and in many cases, save money.

❊ If your budget is tight, let your caterer help you create a low cost, yet delicious menu. The challenge of presenting a beautiful meal within budget can be met by a quality caterer.

GUARANTEEING GUIDE

Buffet:

In guaranteeing for a buffet always guarantee 10% less than have positively R.S.V.P.'d. There is always adequate food and you won't get stuck paying for people that do not show up.

Example: If you have a 100 count guarantee 90. Due to unforeseen circumstances there is a typical no-show of 5-10%.(even more in weddings and open houses.) If for some reason you end up with 95 the buffet will still be ample. If you were to guarantee 100, for instance at $15.00 per person, and only 90 show up, you have wasted $150.00. (This is not unusual.)

Sit Down:

In guaranteeing sit-down dinners, the rule is to guarantee 5% less than have positively R.S.V.P.'d. If everyone does show up, which is unusual, the caterer will have plenty of food.

Guaranteeing for weddings and open houses is the most unpredictable of all events. The fall off can be anywhere from 10% to 25%. Even the most formal invitations for these two types of events result in this sort of fall off.

It is highly recommended that you follow up with R.S.V.P. phone calls if you are serving a sitdown dinner at a hotel or banquet hall. Typically, those meals cost between $10.00 and $25.00 so if your guarantee is off by 10-20 meals it will be costly. (These R.S.V.P. calls can be made in a few hours by a volunteer crew and the savings will be well worth it. It also serves as a reminder for your event.)

Very formal invitations to events other than weddings and open houses will result in a 95% attendance.

Holiday parties have a high rate of attendance. (During the holidays people seem to fit in all of their social engagements.)

Thank you! to Melissa Christiansen, Park Cafe Catering, Minneapolis, Minnesota for the guaranteeing guide.

TRANSPORTATION FOR SPECIAL EVENTS

Buses are often needed to transport groups involved in celebrations. To accommodate out of town guests, to take guests to out-of-town events, to move groups for progressive parties and for actual "on-the-move" parties. Bus rental companies will also provide the drivers and rarely allow you to drive. They will also provide tour guides if you would like to arrange for mini-tours. In some cases you can serve alcoholic beverages on board, but it varies with companies. As does the smoking policy!

Food, entertainment, and activities are all acceptable, in fact, advisable. Long bus rides to transport guests to the event site are made more enjoyable and actually seem shorter when you provide refreshments and entertainment. Singing, playing games, introducing all of the guests, and sociable conversation will fill the time, but it all has to be organized and directed. A small P.A. system (battery operated) is very helpful for directing activities and making announcements. Then you can just leave the driving to them!

Limousines, once an item of luxury and affluence, are now almost everyday transportation for weddings, anniversary celebrations and special occasions of all kinds. You can use limousines to bring Baby home from the hospital, to take Grandma out for her 80th birthday, or to whisk Junior and his seven high school friends to the prom. And, now the latest craze is for grade school chums to rent a limousine for a "last day of school" ride that will take them all over the neighborhood and probably end up at McDonalds for a graduation feast. So, by riding in a stretch limousine anyone can feel like a celebrity. They are able to sit back, sip a glass of champagne, watch their favorite television show or video, make a quick call on the cellular phone and of course, impress the heck out of someone. It is a very nice touch to any event, because even though there are hundreds of limousines driving around in most towns....the vast majority of people have not ridden in one and no matter how cool they try to act, they will love it.

❋ Gift certificates for limousine rides are great for any special occasion.

❋ More and more, several couples are pooling their funds to hire a limousine for a night of club hopping or attending a gala party. The strict drinking and driving laws and the awareness of the danger of driving while under the influence are the influencing factors in using limousines. Each couple's share of the rental cost is usually less than cab fare for two and a lot more fun.

Vans and RV's are available for rent by the day or weekend. If your out-of-town guests number under 20 you will find this a good solution. The driver needs only a regular drivers licence so he/she could be a college student who can use the off time to study if you hire him for the entire weekend. Just call your local car rental service that mentions vans in their ad. It is usually between $60.00 and $75.00 per day, plus what you pay the driver. Providing transportation for your guests is a very hospitable gesture and it will take away the need to be concerned about their being lost or late.

Security Precautions: Unfortunately, there is a possibility of burglaries when your family is in and out of the house for a wedding weekend. Hire someone, if necessary, to come in and housesit while you are away. It will set your mind at ease and prevent any foul play.

Notes & Numbers

~ *Chapter* ~

BABY AND BRIDAL BASHES

Baby and wedding showers are also being planned with themes and schemes. The celebration of these events has far surpassed the days of a few ladies getting together to shower the bride or mother-to-be with useful gifts. Couples showers are very popular, to include the men in the festivities.

Baby Shower Ideas

✳ *Everyone's Expecting* All of the guests dress as pregnant ladies and the food and activities are suitable for expectant mothers.

✳ *Kiddies Party* This time the guests dress as little kids and all of the activities and food are geared for tots.

✱ *Learning and Education* (gifts and games with intelligence, teaching, or testing.) Books, educational toys, subscriptions and gift certificates to museums or classes.

✱ *Nursery Rhymes* (all gifts and activities must come from a rhyme) Hickory Dickory Dock, gives us the idea for a baby alarm clock (is that redundant??), Winken, Blinken & Nod, (baby sleepers), Little Miss Muffet (bowl and spoon) and so forth.

✱ *Song Titles* (gifts and activities center around "baby" songs) Baby Face (mirror) Baby it's Cold Outside (snowsuit) My Baby Just Cares for Me (baby carrier), and more for the creative mind to discover.

"Couples" Themes

New Parents Survival Kit Party. Everyone brings gifts like ear plugs, Excedrin, instruction books, pacifiers—(for Mom and Dad), subliminal tapes, Nodoz and gag gifts like glasses with windshield wipers.

The more serious gifts are pampering-type gift certificates for dinners, limos, movies, cleaning services, massages or gym passes, babysitting time and home cooked meals delivered and served.

An activity for this party: Each guest writes a helpful hint on a 3X5 index card. These hints can be serious or hilarious and will be read aloud.

Set up a flip-type photofile holder for the collection of cards so that the new "folks" can refer to it handily and quickly.

Note: Everyone loves to win the money in a baby arrival pool. Each person puts in from $1.00 to $5.00 along with their guess as to the day and hour of the babies birth. The person guessing closest to the actual date and time wins the pool. In the event that no one guesses within 10 hours of the birth time, the pool goes to open the baby's first savings account.

Another his 'n' hers shower idea is a *Family Album Party.* Guests are invited to participate by bringing a gift that will help the couple document the birth, early days and nights of the newborn's life.

Invitation: A Polaroid picture of a poster with the invitation written on it accompanied with a complete instruction sheet.

Suggested gifts: As a group: Give either a down payment toward a camcorder, Polaroid camera with a supply of film or a tape recorder and tapes.

Individual gifts: scrapbooks, geneology book of family tree how-to's, picture frames, gift certificates at the photo shop or for a photo session.

Plug: Proex has a very professional and reasonable studio setup which provides excellent photos and inexpensive processing. Secret: I had my professional (back of the book) photo taken at Proex. I think they do a great job.

Game: Remind each guest to bring one of their baby pictures (at least one year old,) with their name written on the back. Collect and post those snapshots for all to see. Write a number over each photo so that each player can try to match the baby photos faces to the grownups'. This will be good for a lot of laughs and will be a real challenge.

More fun: Make a video tape of guests wishing special things for the new baby. They can tell funny stories about the parents and the really "old" pals can describe the Mommy and Daddy when they were kids. These little dramatic offerings can be in poetry, song or theatrical playlet. Both parents and child will enjoy this zany documentary.

Memories for baby: Take Polaroid photos of each couple for an "important people" scrapbook for the baby. It is fun to sit and page through the book and teach the child the names that go with the photos.

Decorations: Balloons, streamers, posters of photography supplies or products, old cameras or photography equipment and brochures or books on film or photography. Your local photo supply store should be a good resource for this stuff.

Wedding Shower Ideas

I am all for the "his and her" type showers because the groom gets left out of a lot of planning for a wedding. This gives him a chance to get involved and be part of the fun. It is an opportunity for everyone to meet each other, too, since the in-laws are usually invited to these parties.

These pre-nuptual celebrations are very popular and can be quite zany and frivolous. It is a time to spoof the institution of marriage and honoring the happy couple while adding to the excitement of their upcoming commitment. It is an opportunity to alleviate some of the stress and anxiety that invariably mounts before such an important event. Through fun, laughter and opening up with friends and family, the happy couple can shed some tension and normal apprehension.

Theme ideas are endless. The couple and their special interests, talents, occupations, habits, physical characteristics or quirks are all open game for setting a theme. Persons giving these parties are usually good friends of the bride and groom, so they have no problem coming up with a theme, although sometimes a theme is not readily obvious.

Some Examples:

✳ If the couple is involved in any sports activity you can play on that. Jogging, aerobics, biking, or skating are all activities in which most people can participate and would make a good theme for a party. Guests dress in appropriate gear and are taken out for a jog, bike ride, a skate or put through aerobic paces. Trivia games and videos of the sport, instructions, contests and prizes are all fair play for this type of event. It is a starter theme that can be simplified or elaborated) n a very casual atmosphere, which is popular.

✳ The groom was a lawyer, the bride a musician. The party was labeled *Barristers on Broadway* and was a courtroom takeoff of a musical comedy. The guests were given the role of one of the courtroom cast (judge, jury, bailiff, etc.) Defendant and plaintiff, of course were the guests of honor. All were given scripts for a mini-production. Food and beverage were served during "recesses". Gifts were "evidence" presented to the court. Songs such as *Law is a Many Splendored Thing*, *Happy Trials to You* and *What I did for Law* were part of the repertoire. Some very clever hands created this party and it was a huge success. (At least that was the verdict I heard.)

Sample Couples Party Plan

One event I planned was for a couple known for being extremely neat and organized. Both bride and groom had the same traits so it was a natural.

Invitation : It was sent out on a neatly typed index card, with a Rolodex card and post it note attached revealing pertinent information. Each guest was given a different arrival time, so the beginning of the party would, of course, be orderly.

Gifts: Organizational aids such as closet accessories, date books, clocks, file folders and photo albums. Every room of the house was considered: kitchen, bathroom, den, patio and bedroom.

Decorations: Organizational items like file folders, calendars, day planners, message slips and household items such as silverware drawer organizers, shoe racks, bathroom shower caddies (even automobile items) were used for decorations, table serving ware and favors.

Silly Stuff: As the bride-to-be neatly opened the gifts, the groom-to-be fastidiously filled out an index card with the name of the giver and a description of the item. He promptly filed the cards alphabetically into a file box for use in sending thank you notes. This was typical of their highly organized behavior.

More Silly Stuff: As the guests arrived they were handed a schedule of events, minute by minute and we actually stayed with the schedule pretty much. When it came time to go through the buffet line, everyone lined up in alphabetical order, by last name. I must say, they were very organized (Hysterical, but organized)

How Silly Can You Get? A humorous highlight was when everyone was required to police the area. They picked up trash and straightened up the room to the direction of a drill sergeant, whistle, clipboard and all!

This was a perfect example of how a theme can be carried out, in a highly exaggerated way, but the fun and laughter was evidence of its' success.

❊ *Be careful when spoofing people, though. Sometimes they might be sensitive about certain quirks. The best thing to do is to run a theme by the guests of honor before you start your plans.*

❊ *Remember:* In all shower or couples party planning, arrange for a video camera and operator to capture all those planned or spontaneous, irreplaceable moments of high spirited fun and good wishes.

Notes & Numbers

226

~*Chapter*~

29

Planning Aids

READ EM' AND REAP

I don't claim to know everything about special events, but I do claim to know how to *find* (almost) everything about special events. I keep my eyes peeled for literature, classes, memberships and products that will add to my expertise as a professional planner. My goal in this chapter is to share some of those resources with you so that you, too, can become an expert...if only for one event.

Even though this book you are holding in your hands (with frequency, I hope) is filled with ideas that are "practical" to "off-the-wall" and is compiled to help you fulfill your dreams of events *extraordinaire*, you may want to seek even more ways to increase your event planning skills. Please be my guest.

Books, Magazines, and Literature

Weddings, Anniversaries, Sentimental Times

In most metropolitan markets you will find a nifty little publication called *The Wedding Guide*. It contains up-to-date tips and protocol information along with advertising and coupons from quality vendors in your community that represent the wedding industry. To find out if the Wedding Guide is available in your town call toll free 1-800-477-0142.

Beautiful picture workbooks for planning a wedding by Martha Stewart (who represents K-Mart with non-K-Mart ideas) are available by mail. *The Wedding Planner* keeps you organized with essential check lists, calendars, budget suggestions and handy pockets to hold receipts and samples. This is an elegant effective tool to help you create a lovely wedding. $24.00 (regularly $30.00) plus $2.50 shipping. Call Toll Free 1-800-922-6300.

Some neat little books with more clever ideas to add to my themes, schemes and dreams are published by Brighton Publications, P.O. Box 12706, New Brighton, MN 55112. (612) 636-2220. Authored by Sharon Dlugosch.

Wedding Plans (50 themes)	$9.95
Wedding Hints and Reminders	$7.95

Wedding Occasions	$8.95
Games for Wedding Shower Fun	$5.95
Revised Table Setting Guide	$7.95

*She has two new ones that you can check on called:

Tabletop Vignettes and *Wedding Anniversary Themes*

The expert's expert, Dear Abby, has a booklet you can order called How To Have a Lovely Wedding. You will find answers to questions not asked in the traditional books. Send a business-size, self-addressed envelope, plus check or money order for $3.95 ($4.50 in Canada) to Dear Abby, Wedding Booklet, P.O. Box 447, Mount Morris, IL 61054. (Postage is included).

A gorgeous, four-color magazine called *Best Weddings* may be available in your town, if not now, very soon. Complete with wonderful advice-filled articles, check lists, planning tips and information on new products and services. Brides who register (at no cost) have access to data base resources, prices, people to call for information and advice. This state-of-the-art publishing concept is currently published two times a year in the following cities: Baltimore, Washington, DC, Pittsburgh, Philadelphia and Atlanta. Check for new cities, as they are being added regularly. *1-800-BESTWED.*

Parties and Celebrations

A book of theme party ideas including step-by-step instructions for shopping and planning is called *Parties With Panache,* written by Lennie Rose. Check with your local bookstore. 263 pages, $11.95

A great little free booklet, *Family Reunion Guidebook*, published by Better Homes and Gardens, P.O. Box 10237, Des Moines, IA 50336 gives common sense how-to's for a detail-laden gathering and tells how to track people down and round them up.

To get assistance in your family tree search, contact: The National Archives, Reference Service Branch, Washington, DC 20408-0001 or call (202) 201-5402. If you send a stamped, self-addressed envelope to The National Genealogical Society, Education Division, 4527 Seventeenth St. North, Arlington, VA 22207-2397 they will send you a pamphlet, *Suggestions for Beginners in Genealogy*. You can also find information on this topic at your library or local genealogical society.

When planning a reunion of classmates you can seek the help of professional reunion planners who will help organize the hunt for missing class members, design and implement a successful reunion party and keep your budget on track. For a fee, which is usually saved in expert "shopping" advice, you can have a professional work with you to pull together all the elements for a memorable reunion. The national number to call for your local reunion expert planner is: *National Association of Reunion Planners* (407) 291-2941, out of Orlando, FL

Seventeen Magazine has published a booklet on wedding planning. It costs $1.50. The send-for address is : *Seventeen*, Box 880 Madison Square Post Office, New York, NY 10010

Food for Fifty costs almost $50.00, so you may want to check it out at your local library. It is filled with great recipes designed for large groups. It is published by Shugart-McMillan, 1989 and is available at the B. Dalton stores.

Special Events for Teens

Seventeen Magazine also offers a dandy little booklet called *Party Time!* which includes ideas for themes, decorations, food and entertainment geared to the "about-to-become-adults" crowd. Simply send $1.50 to: Seventeen, Box 880 Madison Square Post Office, New York, NY 10010

Kids are Party People, Too!

Childrens' Parties, Planning Unique and Unforgettable Parties for Your Child by mother and daughter team, Juliette Rogers and Barbara Radcliffe Rogers is filled with creative and thoughtful suggestions for Theme Parties. They've found lots of arts and crafts projects designed to get the kids involved in the stages of planning and creating. Also, there's wonderful color photos of invitations, decorations, costumes, food and games. Other pint-sized people's party topics are covered neatly such as: Kids as Guests, Party-proofing Your Home, Challenged Children, Homemade Invitations, Favors and Prizes. Available in your local bookstore or call : Price Stern Sloan Publishing, Los Angeles, CA. 1-800-421-0892 for the name of the store nearest you.

Fellow Minneapolis, Minnesota author, parent and entrepreneur, Vicki Lansky, has written *Birthday Parties,* a 140 page book of kids' (all ages) birthday party ideas which sells for $6.95 plus $2.25 postage and handling. Send check or money order to: The Book Peddlers, 18326 Minnetonka Boulevard, Minnetonka, MN 55391 or call, 1-800-255-3379.

Note: Vicki Lansky has written books on baby showers, children's parties and child rearing. When you call to order the Birthday Parties book, ask for a brochure on her other books. They are excellent.

Childrens' Party Book: From Tots to Teens, is a 196 page book with a plastic spiral binding published by the Junior League Hampton Roads, Inc. which sells for $10.00 (includes postage and handling). It is a dandy collection of ideas for all kinds of themes, schemes and dreams for kids of all ages. Very well put together by parents. Send check or money order to: Childrens' Party Book, 1310 C. Todds Lane, Dept. Ps, Hampton, VA 23666

How to Become A Professional Planner

For aspiring, semi-professional or full-fledged planners the following publications will prove to be very worthwhile and informative:

Joe Jeff Goldblatt, internationally recognized special event master, who is Executive Producer of The Wonder Company, Washington, DC, has authored a 386-page book called *Special Events, The Art and Science of Celebration* It is the first "textbook" offering for the event industry. By reading it thoroughly you can learn about starting your own business, performing as a fundraising chairman, or planning events for your company or association. This comprehensive volume of how-to's, resources and invaluable, shared experiences of world renowned event professionals is enhanced by colored photos, an awesome glossary and samples of forms. Order through the International Special Event Society at 1-800-344-ISES. The cost is $38.95 plus shipping.

Balloons and Parties Today is a monthly publication for party planners and retailers of party supplies, balloons and flowers. It is "inflated" (I couldn't blow that chance)

[Ed: Next time, try.] with ideas and resources that are available to you. Annual subscription rate is $29.95. Published by Festivities Publications, Inc. (904) 634-1902.

Special Events is a monthly publication for special event professionals. Call for sample copy 1-800-543-4116. You should also request information on The Special Event, a national tradeshow/seminar convention that takes place each January. Special Event pro's from all over the country share their trade secrets.

Special Events: Inside & Out is an excellent 108 page resource for those planning festivals, outdoor events and sports oriented celebrations written by Robert Jackson, the Special Events Coordinator for the 1991 Special Olympics. Formerly an event planner for Disneyland and Walt Disney World. $18.95 plus $2.50 Shipping. Sagamore Publishing, Inc., 1-800-327-5557 or ask for it at your bookstore or library.

Supplies and Services

I am listing some party suppliers that can help you via long distance. If you have a service like this in your town, this section will just serve as a memory jogger and idea file. However, if you do not know of anyone that can provide you with these services, the folks mentioned here are the best in my area (and in the country, I'd bet) and I have had great success working with them. They have contributed tremendously in making my events successful.

Send for their catalogs or samples to vastly increase your resources. Tell 'em Patty Sent You! [Ed: Should they knock three times?]

Party Supplies & Decorations

Andersons' Party Supplies has several great catalogs filled with props, decorations, gift items, invitations, fundraising items, and costume effects for any kind of event. Not only for weddings but for parties and celebrations for personal, business, school, church, civic and association events. Simply call the toll free number and they will send you the catalogs that you request. Even though their main catalog is called the Prom Book, it is loaded with items for all sorts of theme events. In order to get copies of their catalogs, *Weddings, Proms, Spirit and Celebrations* call 1-800-328-9640.

Party Lites have luminaria (candles in paper bags) to light up your walkways, poolside, shoreline, driveway and stairways. 17 colors plus gold and silver bags, 7 designs for any season. Kits include candles, frames and bags. Six for $12.95, dozen for $23.95 (PPD) To receive brochure write to Dept. Ps, P.O. Box 300166, Minneapolis, MN 55403

To create a theme or hide unsightly partitions. spectacular, giant, hand-painted paper backdrops and banners are the answer. *Britten Banners boasts "custom backdrops you can afford"*. They say you can ballpark estimate $2-4 per square foot for most work. Reuseable, reinforced and flameproof. Call toll free 1-800-426-9496 for further information.

234

Archie McPhee has a catalog of goofy, funky, junky, bizarre and silly stuff that will brighten up any event or gift bag. Novelties, antique posters, as well as treasures like golden lifesize pineapples, tiki party lights, lobster claw harmonicas are waiting for you. Write to Archie McPhee at Box 30852, Seattle, WA 98103-0852 for this catalog of eccentric and eclectic items.

For filmland, tinseltown, Hollywood theme parties fill your walls with authentic movie posters and memorabalia from *Rick's Movie Graphics* catalog. He has a huge collection of original posters and some fabulous reproductions of the classics. Send $2.00 to Suite 3E, 1105 N. Main Street, Gainesville, Florida 32601

GTA Party Supplies of Minneapolis is another catalog that offers hundreds of items for carnivals, parties, festivals, fundraisers, and theme parties. Decorations, favors, gimmicks, gifts and costume effects by the dozens or gross for big events. Wholesale prices to the general public. Just call 1-800-328-1226 and order their 70 page catalog.They offer free shipping for orders over $40.00.

Invitations

Diane Designs, Inc. Diane Fisher, designs and manufacturers award winning invitations with nationwide service. Video Taped Mockup service available for fool proof results. Out of Des Moines,Iowa Give her a call at (515)243-5292 for exclusive and custom designs.

First Impressions, Bill Hamm, discovers, designs and creates invitations, announcements and programs for special events of all kinds. They specialize in unique pieces that are mailed in tubes and unusual containers. You can order invitations that are customized or from a special stock collection. For information: 800 Ford Centre, Dept. PS, Minneapolis, MN 55401 or call (612) 338-3837 and speak to Bill Hamm

R.S.V.Positive, extraordinary one-of-a-kind invitations or promotional messages that stand out with originality. Designs include invitations in song recorded on audio or video, printed on surprising surfaces of wearables, edibles, useables and in many cases, laughables.
For catalog and sample contact Roni: (612)-544-7441

Out Of The Envelope, are invitation designs that defy description of their specialness. Mailed in plastic bottles, tubes, see-through containers of all kinds. They're lively and dimensional with miniature items, toys, favors, combined with beautifully printed and decorated papers to make knockout presentations. For brochure or information call: S.Clein, Shirlee Clein, (612) 920-7297. Or write to: 4520 Excelsior Boulevard, St.Louis Park, MN 55416.

Imprint Express, delightful balloon arrangements with special messages imprinted on each balloon. Light as air, they ship beautifully for a great customized greeting that will last for weeks. *Imprint*

Express prices range from $16-25. Call to order, rush service available. Shirlee Clein, 612-920-7297.

Name Tags

PC Nametag Program, is for larger groups gathered for personal or business functions. With it's use you can organize and recognize your guests with super sharp and instantly readable computer printed nametags and placecards. Practical and efficient for reunions, meetings, conventions and parties. Call Topitzes & Associates, of Madison, Wisconsin 1-800-233-9767 for samples and information on this program.(They also have programs for menu planning and party recipes from Bon Appetit.)

Namely, You! Presents a line of exquisite, four color, die-cut name tags for weddings, parties and celebrations. No more, blah"Hello, my name is" nametags. They will also design a very custom name tag for your theme, promotion or event, each one a work of art. For a sample and ordering information, send a self-addressed-stamped envelope (business size) to: Namely, You! 35 Nathan Lane, #309, Plymouth, MN 55441

Favors and Gimmicks

Outrageous Fortunes will fill delicious fortune cookies with the message of your choice. This idea can be used for a promotional item, an invitation or announcement (birth, wedding, engagement). A fun favor for grownups or kids events. They even have a "Lottery Fortune Cookie" that you can use for exciting contests. For pricing information and order sheet: Keefer Food Court, Dept. PS, 326 Cedar Avenue South, Minneapolis, MN 55454.

Creative Cookie, Inc. creates hundreds of wishes in fortune cookies for each particular theme and packages them in a colorful and clever carry-out pail. All the holidays are covered as well as trivia, romantic, for kids only, thank you, congratulations, and many more for great party favors, hostess gifts, prizes. For a nearest dealer call 1-800-451-4005.

Think Big is the name of the catalog that features huge replicas of every day items such as pencils, crayons, scissors, asprins, gatels, tooth brushes and sneakers! Call (800) 487-4244 for catalog – Gallery at 390 West Broadway, N.Y.C.

Guest of Honor Face Masks, are used for an ultimate tribute to an honoree if you believe that duplication is the best form of compliment. With the creation of paper masks made from a photo of the "person of the hour" you can let everyone put on a happy face to greet the guest of honor, either when he/she arrives or at some important point of the event. These masks are black and white or color photocopy enlargements mounted on posterboard, cut to silhouette then attached to a stick/holder. Upon request the masks can be adorned with ribbon bowties, hairbows, jewelry, glasses, or other distinctive-to-design items. Can also be designed as an invitation, menu or program. Send a self-addressed business size enve-

238

lope to *MaskParade Productions,* 47892 Oasis Court, Palm Desert, CA, 92260 and you will receive information sheet.

Treasure Island Party Instructions are available by dropping a note with a check for $5.00 to Your Special Event, Ind. , 35 Nathan Lane, #309, Plymouth, MN 55441.

Snack Plates

A handy plastic plate for buffet serving that has a groove to hold a matching glass or any stem glass or cup. Guests can hold their food and beverage with one hand and eat with the other. Women can even hold their handbag on or under their arm without performing a major juggling feat. For the supplier nearest you, send a self-addressed-stamped envelope to: *Buffet Snackplates,* P.O. Box 65564, St. Paul, MN 55165 or call: 1-800-447-1838, Plastics, Inc. and ask for the distributor in your town. That distibutor can tell you which retailer carries the plate. (or palette, which it resembles)

Chair Covers

A slick slip cover for a folding chair in white plastic with a tuxedo/bow design transforms a room full of ordinary chairs and tables to an elegant setting. Order from *Anderson's Catalog.* (The first listing in this section.)

Confection/Cake Decorating Supplies: The most complete selection of baking, cooking and decorating supplies for creating cakes, candies and elaborate sweet items for your special occasions. Not only is it fun and creative, but you can save money here. *Maid Of Scandinavia Co.*, 3244 Raleigh Avenue, St. Louis Park, MN 55416, Dept. PS, (include $1.00) for catalog of hundreds of items.

For chocolates that are decorative, delicious and designed for you only. Initial, logos, artwork, names, faces, special shapes are all available to make sweets that will be the *Custom Chocolate*,1244 Roselawn, St. Paul, MN 55113, Contact Paul or Janet Schmid, for brochure or special information.

Call Donamae for elegant or cute confectionaries in beautiful containers. Boxes, tins, bags, buckets, baskets and a long list of out-of-the-ordinary containers. They can be customized for fabulous favors and gifts. The Karmel Korn Krunch is as they say, "to die for", it is the specialty of the house and definitely one of *Donamae's Favorites*, 3907 Basswood Road, Minneapolis, MN 55416. Drop a note and she will send you a sample, brochure and photo of her best stuff. Very personalized and thoughtful service.

It's called *Corporate Candy*, but I think any sweetheart can order it. Colorful hard candies with a name or message (up to 20 letters) deliciously imprinted in the center. Given as a favor, a bag or box of these dandy candies will bring pleasure to your guests long after the party ends. Call 1-800-562-4448 (in AL (205)879-GIFT) for samples and prices.

Vintage Clothing and Costumes

It wouldn't be a book of mine (this is my third) if I didn't give a promotional plug to a resource that has been tapped by Disney, Broadway, Hollywood, photographers and creative directors from all over the country. Elsie's Closet Vintage Clothing and Accessories for Women, is one of Minneapolis' claims to fame. She (Elsie Iverson, who started her business when she was sixty) has been running her "closet" for seven years and has provided authentic wardrobes for movies, plays, photo shoots and videos. Give her a call if you are searching for something for a costume party or presentation. She'll send you a photo and if you want she'll pack it up and ship it to you. Her prices are great and she's a kick. It's rumored that she has 5,000 or more hats. (It's because of her that I have written this book. She invited me to my first birthday party. I was born on her 16th Birthday and we've been celebrating our mutual birthdays ever since). Elsie's Closet, 3105 Nicollet Avenue, Minneapolis, MN 55408, (612) 825-5627.

Specialty Entertainment

Spoofs and humorous presentations are the forte of John Klocke, custom comedy writer. For gatherings to honor individuals, couples, or groups you can commission John and Company to create a presentation that is word-for-word customized comedy in the form of vignettes, skits, songs, awards ceremonies and roasts. You will be provided with all that you need to succeed: scripts, music, instruction and if you want, he'll show up to direct. For facts on funny stuff: *John Klocke*, (612)469-3610

On Location Video, Alan & Donna Block, create highly personal and customized videos for use as a gift or presentation at your special event. Working with photos, film, slides, special interviews and your input and theme, they will, with the addition of music, graphics, effects and loving care, produce a work of art for you. These thoughtful video productions make the day and the event. Send them your mixed bag of stuff and it will come back "star-quality" sensational. They've traveled all over the country...to film On Location. Contact them at: (612) 546-3220.

For a speaker, trainer, celebrity, authors & experts, talent of all kinds to liven up your banquet, opening, promotion, commemoration of any sort *Key Speakers Bureau* will assist you in any city. Their collection is extensive and they will find what you are searching for or help you decide what would work. This type of entertainment is especially effective when you need a draw, as in fundraisers and large meetings or conventions. Call Toll Free 1-800-553-9736 Mike Podolinsky for friendly and creative help and some literature on their services.

Interactive Personalities is a high-tech company that features computer generated characters that communicate with guests from a video monitor. They are customized to match your theme, product or image and the scripts they read are written with all of your information, jargon or key names included. State of the art, not inexpensive, but a show-stopping highlight of any event. They have stopped shows all over the world. Contact Dan Yaman or Brent Kauth, (612) 332-7625 for further information.

Flying Saucers, you say. Here is the most incredible "identified object" ever. It soars above the crowd, helium filled, remote controlled, 17 feet in diameter, twinkling lights flashing and as dramatic as anything I've seen in a long time. The Space Oddessy theme sets the perfect background as it's sounds surround the floating disc. There's even a baby *Hystar* (that's what it's called) that floats along with it's Pop. Another technological effect that is for events that are planned with "spectacular" or "extravaganza" in the description. Contact Lynn Heichert, (604)278-0107. The video tape will convince you.

Musical Flashback a groovy new trivia game invented by Bill Gardner of St. Paul, features multiple choice questions spanning the 32-year period from 1955 to 1986 that will lead you to the name of a popular song of that certain month. Great for era parties or just hanging out and showing off what you know. Can be ordered by sending a check or money order for just $15.00 to: Moosehead Enterprises, Dept. PS, P.O. Box 2491, St. Paul, Mn 55102-0491.

Wedding Specials

A great alternative to the traditional wedding ceremony program is being produced by *Unique Ink*, of Eden Prairie, MN. They take your color engagement photo and use it as the cover of the program. The schedule of your ceremony and your bridal party are listed inside while the back cover is reserved for your special message to your guests. High quality four color printing process on deluxe paper. Guests usually discard programs soon after the wedding day but these lovely mementos will be saved forever. For a sample and price list write to: 7605 Equitable Drive, Dept. PS, Eden Prairie, MN 55344

A Legacy of Lace, creates one-of-a-kind bridal garter sets (one to toss and one to keep) with elegant lace(white or ivory), pearls and handmade ribbon rosebuds in 12 stock colors (custom colors available,too) for $29.95 a set. Their other specialty Satin potpourri-filled rose buds personalized with the bride and grooms' names and wedding date make lovely favor items and are priced at 25 for $25.95. You may call for ordering information: 1-612-559-6159.

When the bride kicks off her elegant new shoes to dance the night away – she won't ruin her lovely hosiery since she's wearing her FORMAL SNEAKERS. Lace, ribbon and flowers in coordinated wedding colors adorn crisp white slip-on sneakers. You can order for the whole wedding party... men too! Call Donna at 1-800-323-3819.

fun tips
cute ideas
happy hints
brain storms

THEMES, SCHEMES AND DREAMS

Before we finish, here are a couple of party plans that are among my favorites. One is a theme that was carried out to the limit as far as gimmicks and silliness. The second was a unique and creative concept that made use of an entirely different set of elements.

Baby Bobby's 40th Bash

"He must have been a beautiful baby" was the theme of this baby birthday bash. It featured gimmicks, games and getups guaranteed to take the guests back to their childhood days. The hostess and the guest of honor were fun-loving and adventurous but, most of all, smart when they presented me with a proposed theme, some basic good ideas and a budget, and then,for the most part, gave me the freedom to "go for it." I like that in a client.

Three tickler letters were sent alerting guests to save the date. They were followed by the official invitation, which was a cassette-taped song parody of "You Must Have Been a Beautiful Baby" and a photo of the "bouncing birthday boy" all decked out in diaper and bonnet, sitting in a huge high chair. His and Hers pacifiers tied to blue or pink ribbons completed the party kit invitation.

Another recorded parody greeted the caller on a special R.S.V.P. Voicemail line. It was like taking candy from a baby. [Ed: Grow up, will ya?] The response was almost 100%.

Preparing for this extravaganza felt a little like traveling back in time a few decades [Ed: Few?] as I shopped for, ordered and wrapped toys, games, treats, prizes, decorations, more treats and talents. In the meantime, the guests were having as much fun as I was in preparing their "little outfits" as the invitation instructed. Diapers, Dr. Dentons, Baby Dolls, Bibs and Bonnets came out of the closet for this little party.

The little guys and gals were greeted by brightly costumed "clowning" valet parkers at the end of a balloon-festooned driveway. I took the opportunity to dress up as The Fairy Godmother leading the little guests into the party, reminding them all to behave while giving them their "be sure to be" goody bags.

And the Cuteness Prevailed!

Refreshments: Beverages served in baby bottles and Tommy Tippy cups, junk food and candy treats in buckets, baskets and bowls with a huge old fashioned decorated cake dominating a corner table.

Games: Pin the Tail on the Donkey, Drop the Clothespin in the Milk Bottle, Musical Chairs and Name That Tune.

Amusement and activities: Facepainters, clowns, magicians, contests with prizes and awards supervised by the camp counselors (my guys) dressed in imprinted T-shirts and hats, wielding clipboards and tin whistles.

Favors: The Official High Chair was in a place of honor with a banner hanging behind it that read "Bobby's Pals." Each couple posed in the chair for a Polaroid photo that was presented in a baby blue and pink frame. The goody bags contained bubble blowing stuff, ball and paddle toys, kaleidoscopes, and party favors.

Decorations: The swimming pool was filled with forty inflated plastic birthday cakes (the subtle night lighting made this an awesome scene). Tons (I guess that would be a lot, wouldn't it?) of balloons and streamers, confetti and party signs were hung everywhere.

Special touch: Finger paints (in the hostess interior color scheme) and canvas were provided for the little artists and the result of the nights work was framed and displayed in a place of honor.

The finale of the evening was the viewing of a video production starring "the kid's" friends, family and business associates, each giving him a tasteful (in most cases) and gracious birthday message. We even got an interview with his high school football coach, who very convincingly said, "Bobby Who??"

After extending the curfew several times, the "pooped" (not literally) partyers toddled on home and the crew came in to clean up. The host, hostess and Fairy God-mother agreed that they probably wouldn't be doing that again until Bobby was at least a "teenager."

Treasure Island Hunt

Adding an element of suspense to your event is a fool-proof way to get your guests involved way ahead of the actual starting hour. One of the most successful ways to create this suspense is to plan a theme party and keep most of the important details a secret. The guests will know where and when to meet, what to wear and that is all. What they will be doing and where they will be going is never divulged.

My favorite "mystery" party was a treasure hunt that involved bussing the guests to a local shopping mall where they would compete in a high energy scavenger-type contest. Each team would be challenged to find clues which would be located in shops and kiosks. The guests were instructed to wear tropical attire which suggested several different themes and activities. I learned later that there was great speculation and devious "detectiving" going on to uncover the secret. It was lively and fun for all and increased the number of those that planned to attend. Rumor has it that the most popular guess was that the plans were to go out on a boat trip. The halls were humming with conversation and the planners were under constant pressure to give up the facts for this company party.

After gathering at the designated meeting place, the guests boarded a bus and headed out for the mystery destination. The hosts, lavishly dressed in pirates gear, created quite a scene as they "swashed their buckles" and grandiosely served liquid refreshments. They passed out leis in eight different colors to organize teams. As the bus made its' way to the destination (still unbeknownst to the adventurous and bewildered guests) it suddenly veered off the road to stop in front of a bus shelter. The "dastardly" band of pirates leaped off the bus and promptly began to badger a colorfully dressed bag lady who innocently waited for her bus. The scalawags not only harassed the poor woman but they vigorously grabbed her by the arm and forced her onto the bus. She fought, yelled, kicked, swung her bags at her abductors to effectively complete the ruckus. Undaunted, the Captains "Hook & Crook" shouted instructions to the bus driver "to carry on"!.

As would be expected, the guests were shocked and appalled at this wild kidnapping scene and as the "bagged bag lady" ranted and raved, they clearly did not know whether to laugh or leap. The plot of this mystery thickened when the kidnappee stood suddenly and revealed herself as the official planner and rule maker for the days' event. (I must admit that I looked pretty cute in my three piece lime polyester pantsuit, white crinkly vinyl sandals and dynel wig.) As I finished explaining the rules of the hunt we arrived at the mall. A loud burst of enthusiasm and excitement catapulted the color-coded teams out of the bus, each given their first clue envelope, a map of the mall, game instructions and good luck wishes. Off they raced, 80 restless "natives" determined to be on the winning team.

I'll make a sincere attempt to tell you how this shopping center treasure hunt worked, though it will be a challenge to explain it in a few paragraphs. (You can order complete instructions for this party. See PLANNING RESOURCES, Chapter 29)

After meeting with mall management to explain the concept we obtained permission to hold the hunt there. We provided complete instructions to the shop managers and spoke with each in person to answer any of their questions or concerns. All this accomplished, we designed the game.

✳ Each team's mission was to collect a set of envelopes starting with the clue in their first envelope which, when deciphered, would reveal the name of the shop where their second envelope could be found. (Each envelope had a letter of the alphabet written on it and a qualifying set would spell out their company name.)

✳ The first team to finish and return to the bus would be clocked in as the grand prize winners with the next five teams taking runner-up prizes.

✳ The hunt route was designed to take the teams on a path that would require the longest distance between clue sites. *Example:* Clue #1 directed them to a shop on the first floor in the southwest corner then clue #2 sent them to a store in the northeast corner of the third floor, etc.

✳ There were 100 stores in the center and since each of the eight teams needed to collect 12 envelopes (each teams clues were entirely different) nearly every store was involved.

✳ A "set-up crew" distributed the envelopes to all of the shops with the instruction that a player would come in and ask *"Do you have an envelope for me?"* and at the same time show their previous clue envelope to the shop manager. If the envelope they showed was the right color the store manager could pass along the envelope he held but if the players' envelope was the wrong color the team would get a quick "No" for an answer. (In most cases the teams would have the right store, because the clues although cryptic they were not terribly difficult.)

✳ In addition to regular retail shops, the clues directed every team to specialty kiosks where they were required not only to collect a clue envelope but to also collect proof that they performed such feats as posing for a photo with a celebrity cardboard cutout, (Polaroid photo) recording a song on the Karaoke Singing Machine,(cassette tape) and buying a mylar doubloon, oops, I mean balloon.[Ed: She hasn't got a clue.] The breathless and parched pillagers were also led to one of the malls restaurants where they were "forced" to down a cup of a specially created brew, "Pirate's Potable". All in all, they had an experience to treasure forever.

The Saturday afternoon shopping crowd was quite amused to see grownup persons stampeding up and down escalators, in and out of shops, waving maps, envelopes, and high-flying balloons. (This group of "super sleuths" happened to be a sales staff so the competitive spirit was strong, bordering on aggressive.)

After the last team was clocked in the exhausted explorers boarded the bus which returned them to the original meeting spot, that happened to be the location of the festive island luau finale and awards ceremonies. The entire escapade was videotaped so that the tape could be shown at the party. Several of the losing teams contested the ethics of the winning teams so the tape was very valuable in determining the validity of the accusations. The grand finale was sheer bedlam and needless to say, held an abundance of raucous fun and laughter. After the mates' "ayes and nays" were counted, the Island Treasure Hunt was proclaimed a hit.

~*Chapter*~

WORK SHEETS, PLAY SHEETS

Now that you have read through the book, you will want to start planning your next event. The forms in this chapter will be helpful to you in your precise and efficient planning. The sheets are set up so that you can make copies on your copy machine and they will be 8 1/2 X ll for easy use in a three ring notebook. Or if you like, use them right in the book. (I would suggest that you make some copies before you do that.)

At the end of each chapter (where it merits) you will find a sheet for notes and numbers. As you do planning research the notes that you make will create a valuable directory for your event and celebration discoveries. You might want to write in pencil to allow for updates on contacts or prices.

The postal guide is current, but as I tap away at the keyboard, the news informs me that the postal rates will change. Just make your changes as they occur. The size requirements and limitations should remain the same.

Have fun, be organized (are those two incompatible?).

And if you come up with anything incredible that you think I should know about, please write and tell me about it. Who knows, maybe the next edition will include your idea. If I use your idea in our next "Idea Book" I will print your name and send you two free copies of the book.

I know that there are creative-genius-party-planners out there that could skate circles around me. I'd love to meet you all. If you drop a line we can also put you on our list of "call these people when you are in their town" to use in our book tour. You might just hear from us.

Also, if you are an aspiring event planner and would like to have a copy of our booklet, "Do I Really Want to Be a Party Planner?". It is 10 pages and answers the questions about my job that I get asked on a daily basis. Send $3.00 to cover postage and handling costs and we will do our best, through this little publication, to help you get started.

What Can You Mail For One Stamp?

Add 10c postage to
Envelopes which do not
Meet these specs.

Largest Envelope: 6–1/2" x 11"
Minimum Thickness: .007"
Weight: 1 oz.
Oddball Envelopes: Divide height
of envelope by width. If your
answer is at least 1.3" but 2.5"
or less, it is an OK size.

Largest Post Card Which Can Be Mailed: 4–1/4" x 6"

6 in.

Smallest Piece Which Can Be Mailed (Exception: 1/4" or Fatter)

5 in.

3.5 in.

4–1/4 in.

Post Card: 3–1/2 in. X 5 in. up to 4 in. X 6 in.
Not less than .007 in. thick

MASTER

CARD #	DUTY	√	DELEGATED TO
1			
2			
3			
4			
5			
6			
7			
8			
9			
10			
11			
12			
13			
14			
15			
16			
17			
18			
19			
20			
21			
22			
23			
24			
25			

(Place book flat in copier to

PLANNING SHEET

CATEGORY	

make additional worksheets) ←

RESOURCES

Occasion _____ **Date**_____

Event_____

Site of Event _____

Item	Company	Phone
Invitations		
Caterer/Food		
Entertainment		
Rental Equip.		
Decorations		
Photographer/ Video		
Gifts/ Favors		
Staff (bartenders)		
Valets		
Talent		

(Place book flat in copier to

WORKSHEET

Time _____

Where _____

Contact _____ Phone _____

Contact	Notes

make additional copies)

♣ ♦ ♥ ♠   ♣ ♦ ♥ ♠   **The Beverage Bar**   ♣ ♦ ♥ ♠   ♣ ♦ ♥ ♠

Having a party? The Beverage Bar can quickly make or break the budget. Here are some key guidelines to follow when planning a two-hour cocktail party. Consider the time of year, your guests' preferences.

QUANTITIES FOR DIFFERENT NUMBERS OF GUESTS

ITEM	8 to 10 guests	15 guests	25 guests	50 guests
Bourbon: (fifth)	"on hand"	1 optional	1 optional	1
Gin: (fifth, seasonal)	"on hand"	1 optional	1 optional	2
Rum: (fifth)	"on hand"	1 optional	1 optional	1
Scotch (fifth)	1	1	1 to 2	2 or 3
Vodka (fifth)	1	1 to 2	1 to 2	2 or 3
Red Wine (750 ml)	1		4	7
White Wine (750 ml)	2	3	8	14
Beer (12 ounces)	6	8	12	24
Mixers: (tonic; seltzer)	1 liter	1 liter	3 liters	5 liters
Sparkling/Mineral Water	1 liter	3 liters	4 liters	8 liters
Soft Drinks (cola, diet soda, non-cola)	1 liter	2 liters	3 liters	6 liters
Orange Juice	1 quart	1 quart	2 quarts	2 quarts
Tomato Juice	1 quart	1 quart	1 quart	2 quarts
Limes and/or Lemons	3	6	8	12
Orange	3	6	8	12
Ice (pounds for drinks)	5	15	25	50
Glasses	25	35	60	125
Cocktail Napkins	35	60	100	200

Optional items: Cherries, Celery Sticks, Fresh Pineapple Spears, Swizzle Sticks.

Self Magazine, May 1988

Index

3X5 Cards
    Planning 12
50th wedding anniversary 137
90's Trends 179
    Activities 180
    Attire 180
    Charitable Events 184
    Decor 180
    Family Involvement 184
    Food and Beverage 181
    Interesting Guests 183
    Potluck How-to 181
    Sensory Appeal 182
    Sentimentality 182
Acknowledging Contributors 164
Adventure Club 27
advertising specialties 125
American Institute of Floral Designers 196
Andersons' Party Supplies 234
Apres Party and Tent Rentals 210
Archie McPhee 235
Artistic Greetings, Inc. 188
Association of Bridal Consultants 196
Auction Items 163
Autograph and Artists Party 110
Baby Bobby's 40th 245
baby-sitting 101
Balloon Bouquets 190
Balloons 123
    Arches 128
    Centerpieces 124
    Drops 126
    Fill Space 128

Guest Rooms 128
hanging 124
Hot Air Balloons
    Advertising 126
Imprinted 124, 236
Jeweltones 125
Sculptures 123
Stuffing 125
Tubes 123
Weights 124
wishes 135
With lights 40, 129
Balloons and Parties Today 232
Ballroom Dance Course 89
Banners
    Customized 131
    Sculptured 131
Banquet Space
    Interview
        No Food & Beverage 209
        With food and beverage 207
Bar Chart 260
Barbershop Quartets 88
baseball cards 188
beauty make-overs 101
Best Weddings 229
Big League Cards, Inc. 188
Birthday Parties, 231
Boats 48
Bon Appetit 237
Britten Banners 234
Broadway Shows 18
Budget
    Decorations & Signage 56
    Distribution Philosophy 55

Entertainment 57
Food and Beverage 56
Gifts, Favors 57
invitations 55
location 55
Name Tags, Place Cards 57
Principles 58
Sample 54
buffet line 100
    pitfalls 175
Buffet Service, 166, 167
    Bars
        burger & brat bar 170
        crepes Bar 170
        Fondue Bar 170
        ice cream sundae bar 170
        pancake, waffle bar 170
        Pasta Bar 170
        peanut butter bar 170
        Potato Bar 170
        Salad, 169
    clean up 174
    for fifty 173
    Grazing 168
        Ethnic Foods 169
    Caterers, Guaranteeing Guide 214
    leftover food 174
    Location 175
    Monitoring Food 176
    open houses 173
    passing food 174
    tidy naps 174
Buffet Snackplates, 239
buffet tables 38
    decorations 170

    contemporary 172
    themes 172
    vintage 171
    casual 171
Bullock's By Appointment 189
Buses 215
    Entertainment 215
calendar, personalized 188
Caricaturists 84
carnival talent 92
Casual atmosphere, formal occasion 40
Catalogs 234,235
caterers
    family recipes 213
    Guaranteeing Guide, 214
    interview 211
Celebrities 90, 183
Celebrity Participation, 163
Celebrity Photo 87
chair covers 40, 239
Charitable Events 184
Childrens' Parties 231
Childrens' Party Book
    From Tots to Teens 232
Christmas in July 17
Computer Printouts 85
Corporate candy, 240
costume parties 107
    autographs & artists 110
    rock around the clock 111
    themes listed 113
    wedding re-enactment 112
    weekend get-a-way 111
Costumed Characters 87

costumes, 107
   where to find 108
Creative Cookie, Inc. 238
Crepes Bar 170
Cruise Ship 18
Custom Chocolate, 240
custom gift services 189
custom puzzle 68
customized wine label 102
dance floor 39
Days Inn of America 42
Dear Abby, 229
Decorations 122
   Balloon ideas 128
   Balloons 123
   Banners 234
   chair covers
      plastic 239
   In Storage 148
   Luminaries 234
   Movie items 235
   Table 124
Diane Designs, Inc. 235
directional help 96
dividers 38
doggie bags 174
Donamae's Favorites, 240
Dream trips, 188
Dress code 107
dress-up clothes, 107
EconomyEvents 153
edible gifts 102
Elsie Iverson 241
Elsie's Closet 241
engraved 102

Entertainment 84
    Ballroom Dance Class 89
    Barbershop Quartets 88
    Celebrities 90
    Comedy Writing 241
    Computer Generated Characters 243
    Costumed Characters 87
    Fortune Tellers 87
    Gambling Tables 89
    Helium Flying Saucers
        Hystar 243
    Karaoke machine 91
    magicians, mimes, jugglers 92
    Silhouette cutters 90
    Speakers 242
Eras 19
Erma Bombeck, 165
ethnic foods 169
Event budget 53
    Sample 54
Event Plan
    Cake Concept 9
event schedule 30
event sites 36
    Helping The Homeless
        Day's Inn 42
    less than perfect 38
        Casual Atmosphere/Formal Occasion 40
        Formal Decor/Casual Event 40
        Large Group/Small Space 39
        small group/large space 38
    San Francisco
        Cable Car 41
    selection 37
Face Painters 85

Family Game Night 203
Family Involvement 184
family picnics 203
Family Reunion Guidebook, 230
Favors
    Birthdate Certificates 102
    Face Masks
        MaskParade Productions 238
    Fortune Cookies 237, 238
        Creative Cookie, Inc. 238
        Outrageous Fortunes 237
Festivities Publications, Inc. 233
Finger paints 247
First Impressions, 236
Fish For A Day 190
fishing trip 189
Flying Saucers, 243
Fondue Bar 170
Food
    Cake Decorating Supplies 240
    Custom Chocolates 240
    customized candy 240
    gift confections
        Karmel Krunch
            DonaMae's 240
Food for Fifty 230
Formal decor, casual event 40
formal wear 107
formal sneakers 244
Fortune Tellers/ 87
Fotozines/Success 188
Frame that Tune 190
Fun in Frisco 41
Fund Raisers 161
    Celebrity Participation 163

Planning with 3x5 Cards 161
Volunteer Coordinator 162
volunteer organization 162
Volunteer Recruitment 162
Fund Raising Events
Acknowledging Contributors 164
Auction Items 163
invitations 163
Selling Tickets 163
Sponsorship 164
Tickler Postcards 163
Gala Wedding Re-enactment 112
Gambling 89
Games
Musical Trivia Records 243
Musical Flashback 243
Games for Wedding Shower Fun 229
Garbage Can Dinner
Potkuck 176
Gatsby 18, 20
gift certificate 142
gift certificates
limousines 216
Gift shopping 142
Gifts 185
Balloon Bouquets 190
Big League Cards, Inc. 188
Birth Date Calendar 188
Bullocks Gift Service 189
Celebrity Frame 187
Charitable 95
Customized Greeting Cards
Hallmark 191
Disney Stuff 190
Dream Trips 188

Fishing Trips 189
International Star Registry 189
LoveLetters, Inc. 186
Memoirs Written 189
Record Album Frames 190
Song Sendsations, Inc. 187
Success Magazine cover 188
TimeKeepers 186
Grazing 168
Themes 169
Greeters 98
GTA Party Suppliers 235
guaranteeing 214
Guest Comfort
Duration of event 103
Go-home Guide 105
Greeters 98
Hotel Room Gifts 102
Personalized 102
invitations 95
Light and Sound 102
Name Tags, Place Cards 97, 99
Out of town Guests 101
Place Cards 99
Searchlights 98
Snack Plates 100
Special Seating 100
Valet Parking 100
Weddings
Receiving Lines 104
Reception site 103
Receptions 104
guest gifts 102
Guest of Honor Face Masks 238
Hallmark 191

handicapped guests 99
handwriting reader 87
Hard to Find Gifts 142
Helpful Hospitality Hints 95
Hobbies 19
Holiday Helpers 140
    Decorating Party 142
    Easy Entertaining 141
    Furniture Protection 144
    Gift Certificates 142
    Hard to find Gifts 142
    Hiring Help 144
    Kids 141
    Parties for Chores 141
    Pet Care 144
    Postcard Greetings 143
    Potluck dinners 140
    Recycled cards 143
    Shopping Times 143
    Stain Removers 144
    Two Party System 141
Holidays 19, 140
hospitality 94
hotel ballrooms 37
How To Have a Lovely Wedding 228
Hystar 243
Ice Cream Socials 20
Ice Cream Sundae Bar 170
Idea Book
    Submit ideas 254
Imprint Express 236
Instant Weekend Get-Away 111
Instructions
    Treasure Island Party 239
Interactive Personalities 243

International Society of Meeting Planners 196
International Special Events Society 196, 233
International Star Registry, The 198
invitations 60
  attachments 63
  business 69
  calligraphy 77
  cartoon contest 68
  custom designs 235, 236
  designers 79
  Diane Designs, Inc 235
  directions 96
  First Impressions 236
  gimmicks 62
  gimmicks A-Z 69
  hand delivering 80
  handwriting fun 67
  jigsaw puzzle 67
  labels 76
  little tips 77
  magic theme 66
  mailing sample 75
  mailing times 78
  maps & directions 80
  Mexican Fiesta 64
  mystery party 65
  original 62
  Out Of the Envelope 236
  out of towners 75
  papers 63, 75
  postcards 80
  R.S.V.P. 65
  R.S.V.Positive 236
  recycling calligraphy 75
  regrets only 79

roaring twenties 64
singles party 65
split personality 68
stamps 76
stock 61
the perfect one 81
unique containers 63
voice mail 66
island luau 252
Italian 17
Joe Jeff Goldblatt, 232
jugglers 92
Junior League Hampton Roads, Inc. 232
Karaoke (Sing Along) Machine 91
Karmel Korn Krunch 240
Keefer Food Court 237
Key Speakers Bureau 242
kids
    parties 200
        costume 201
        neon 202
        paint & sign 202
        sites 203
Large group in small space 39
leftover cakes 175
    take-home cartons 174
Legacy of Lace 244
Light 102
Limousine Scavenger Hunt 28
Limousines 215
    Pooling 216
LoveLetters, Inc. 186
Luau 17
magicians 92
Maid Of Scandinavia Co. 240

Mardi Gras 18
Mary Kay 101
MaskParade Productions, 238
Master Planning Sheet 257
Mate Hunting Theme Parties 29
Meeting Planners International 196
memoirs 189
memorial ceremony 135
merit awards, 189
Mexican Fiesta 18
mimes 92
mini-city tours 101
money machine 89
Mood Lighting 33
Musical Flashback 243
musical tributes 182
name tags 97, 99, 116
    alternatives 118
    computerized 119, 237
    Customized
        Namely, You! 237
    Games 119
    Ideas 118, 119
    placement 118
    reunions 117
    weddings 117
Namely You! 237
National Association of Balloon Artists. 196
National Association of Catering Execs. 197
National Association of Reunion Planners 197, 230
Novelties
    Catalogs 234
Occupations 19
On Location Video, 242
Open House Buffet 173

Out Of The Envelope, 236
Out-of-town guests 101
Outdoor Expeditions 188
Outrageous Fortunes 237
Palette serving tray 169
Pancake, Waffle & French Toast Bar 170
Parties on the Move 48
Parties With Panache 229
Party Lites 234
Party Planner Booklet 254
party planners 193
Party Pooling 146
    Application Form 148
    Examples 151
    Fund raising groups 151
    Plans 147
    Setting it up 147
    Teenagers Involvement 150
Party Potty 51
party room 37
Party Supplies 234, 235
Party Time! 231
Pasta Bar 170
PC Nametag Program 237
Peanut Butter Bar 170
Peanuts comic strip 191
People
    Special 5
Personalities 90
personalized song parody 187
Pets Protection 144
Photo Buttons 86
Photoballoons. 125
Place cards 99
    Rules 119

Plan
  Cake Analogy 9
Planners
  Non-Professional 194
  Professional
      Associations 196
      Interviewing 195
  Professional Fees 194
  Vendors Associated 194
Planning Resources 227
  Booklets
      Geneology 230
      teens 231
  Books
      kids parties 231
      Parties 229
      Weddings 228
  Decorations 234
  Kids Parties 231
  Professional
      Special Events 233
  Professional Planning 232
  Reunions 230
  Supplies 233
  Weddings
      Seventeen Magazine 230
Planning worksheets 256
plastic birthday cakes 247
Plastics, Inc. 239
Poems, songs or skits 136
Polariod photo 247
Postal Chart 255
postcard greetings 143
Potato Bar 170
potluck 140, 181

dinner ideas 181
private banquet rooms 37
private halls 37
Professional event planners
    Hiring 193
psychic 87
R.S.V.Positive 236
rating an event 1
    Activities 3
    decorations 1
    Food & Beverage 2
    Music & Entertainment 2
    people 1
Readers 87
Renaissance 18
renewing their vows 136
Rental Equipment
    Bar Height Table 39
    Interview 207
    Party Potty 51
Rental Tips 207
Resources Worksheet 258
Revised Table Setting Guide 229
Rick's Movie Graphics catalog 235
roaring twenties buffet 172
roasts 182
RV's 216
S. Clein, 187
Safari 20
Schedule
    Keeper 34
    Open Houses 33
    Printed Program 34
searchlight 98

Seating
    Handicapped, elderly 120
seating chart 120
Security Precautions 217
sensory 182
    Presentations
        Roasts 183
Sentimental Journey 138
Sentimentality 134
    Anniversary Gifts 137
    Baby Gifts 135
    Book of Life 136
    Going Away Gifts 138
    invitations 135
    Sing Along 138
    Songs, Skits 136
    Taped Messages 136
    Toast & Roasts 137
    Wedding Ceremonies 136
seving plate 100
Serving Plates
    Buffet Snack Plates 228
Showers 219
    Baby
        Couple Themes 220
        Decorations 220
        Games 220
        Gifts 221
        invitations 221
        Photos 221
        Pool Betting 221
        Theme 219
        Themes 220
    Couples
        Party Plan 224

Wedding 223
   Themes 223
signage 97
Signs 130
   Marquee Lighted 130
   Neon 130
Silhouettes 90
sing-along machine 91
Skiing in the Alps 18
Small group in large space 38
Snack Plates 100
SongSendsations, Inc. 187
sound 102
Space Savers
   Bar Height Table 39
Special Events 233
Special Events: Inside and Out 233
Special Events, The Art and Science
   of Celebration 232
Sponsorship 164
stain remover kit 144
sterling silver tray engraved 138
Success Magazine 188
Suggestions for Beginners in Genealogy 230
table numbers 119
Tabletop Vignettes 229
tarot card 87
tea leaf 87
Themed events 22
Themes
   Adventure Club 27
   Boats 49
   Kids Parties
      All-Kids 210
   Limousine Scavenger Hunts 28

Mate Hunting Parties 29
Museum sites 46
Non-Party 21
Safari 20
Same Color 20
setting 15
Trains 49
Wedding Showers 222
weddings 17
Thrift stores 108
Think Big Catalog 238
Time Trivia 111
TimeKeepers 186
toasts 137
Topitzes & Associates, 236
tour guides 101
tournament prizes 189
Trains 49
Transportation
    Buses
        Alcohol 215
    vans 101
Treasure Island Hunt 249
Treasure Island Party Instructions 239
Tuxedoes 109
Twinkle lights 41
two party system 141
Unique Events Sites 44, 49
    Barn or farm 45
    Boats & Yachts 48
    List 47
    Mansions 46
    Museums and Zoos 46
    Office building Atriums 47
    Precautions 50

Selecting 45
Victorian Houses 46
Warehouses 45
Unique Ink, 244
Unique sites
how to find 45
Valet Parking 100
Vans 217
vans or mini-buses 101
Vicki Lansky 231
Victorian 17
Victorian photographer 87
Video
Baby Showers 222
Video Presentations
Customized
On Location Video 242
vintage clothing
mail order
Elsie's Closet 241
vintage clothing stores 108
Walt Disney Catalog 190
Wedding Anniversary Themes 228
Wedding ceremonies 136
Wedding Hints and Reminders 228
Wedding Guide 228
Wedding Occasions 229
Wedding Parties
Video 135
Wedding Plans (50 themes) 228
Wedding Planner 228
Wedding Themes
Alpine 18
Broadway Shows 18
Cruise Ship 18

    Era's 19
    Gatsby 18
    Hobbies 19
    Holidays 19
    Italian 17
    Luau 17
    Mardi Gras 18
    Mexican Fiesta 18
    Occupations 19
    Renaissance 18
    Same Color 18
    Victorian 17
Weddings
    Formal Sneakers 244
    Garter Sets 244
    Photo Programs 244
    Reception delays 103
Wonder Company, The 232
yachts 48

SPECIAL! SPECIAL!

Quantity book prices for promotion or fundraising: You may purchase quantities of this book at a reduced cost for use in promotional projects or fundraising campaigns. Complete the form below and send it along with your business card to:

Your Special Event
35 Nathan Lane #309
Plymouth, MN 55441

Please send quantity purchase information to:

Name   Phone

Address

City   State   Zip

Business Organization

ORDER FORM

Exciting and unique items for celebrations!! In the all new *WEDDINGS, PARTIES, AND CELEBRATIONS CATALOG.*

Plan a perfect party from your home! No more hours of shopping and running around.

- Party Goods • Decorations • Books
  - Wedding Supplies • Invitations
- Name Tags • Personalized Gifts • Favors

Send to: **Catalog**
             35 Nathan Lane #309
             Plymouth, MN 55441

To receive catalog, complete and return form with $1.00 shipping and handling.

Name   Phone

Address

City   State   Zip

Notes & Numbers

Notes & Numbers

Notes & Numbers

Notes & Numbers

Notes & Numbers

Notes & Numbers

Notes & Numbers

Notes & Numbers

Notes & Numbers

Notes & Numbers

Notes & Numbers

Notes & Numbers